not of this...
world

by Mark Matlock

This book belongs to Ambassador...

NOT OF THIS WORLD

Scripture verses are taken from the Holy Bible: New International Version, copyright © 1973, 1978, 1984 International Bible Society. Used by permission of Zondervan Bible Publishers.

Shepherd Catalog number 2300
Printed in the United States of America ISBN 0-923417-69-9

First Printing: September 1998

Editor and Publication Director: Wayne Peterson
Art Director: Russ Chilcoat
Graphic Designers: Russ Chilcoat and Shatrine Weik
Photography: Russ Chilcoat and Shatrine Weik
X-Ray Photography: Alice Wells
Author Assistant: Greg Wilson
Proofing: Nancy Gibson
Devotionals in Appendix B: Christopher Lyon
Mostly True Stories: Copyright of Mark Matlock

SHEPHERD MINISTRIES
2221 WALNUT HILL LN
IRVING, TX 75038-4410
ph 972.580.8000
tf 800.646.8336
fx 972.580.1329

e-mail: SHEPHERD@SHEPMIN.COM
web site: WWW.SHEPMIN.COM

About the Author

For nearly eight years, Mark has ministered full time to youth pastors and students across the United States using his unique teaching style incorporating solid Biblical truth with humor, storytelling and illusions. In his travels he has spoken face to face with nearly one million students nationwide.

Mark Matlock is the president and founder of WisdomWorks Ministries in Irving, Texas. WisdomWorks was designed to effectively and creatively teach students of all ages to live life from God's perspective. WisdomWorks is most known for their Internet site (www.wisdomworks.org) incorporating interactive media, devotionals, question and answer forums, Dr. Dares Kitchen, QuickTime® videos and other exciting experiences to help students live lives pleasing to God.

Mark Matlock is an ordained minister and the author of several books, videos, and audio tapes. Mark resides in Irving, Texas with his wife Jade and their two children Dax and one who remains to be born (Jan 1999) as of this printing.

Mark Matlock
PRESIDENT

WisdomWorks Ministries
P.O. Box 166317
Irving, TX 75016-6317
(972) 871-0274

Using This Journal

Not of this World is a study and discussion tool for individuals, one-on-one counseling, youth groups, weekend conferences, seminars and week-long camps.

This journal will challenge the thinking student who is looking for answers about his purpose in life, and how he can maximize his relationship with God in this world. It is an excellent resource for the youth leader who is seeking to develop the faith and commitment of students.

Scripture passages in this manual are highlighted in bold print to call attention to their importance and to make them stand out within the pages. The Bible is our ultimate resource in life and is the heart of this study.

The questions are designed to motivate thoughtful discussion, make significant points clearly understandable and to apply Scripture to the individual in current experience. Sections of text printed in colored boxes give additional insights, illustrations, and other parenthetical learning helps. The projects are useful for deeper exploration into the topics and to encourage application in life.

The planned progression of this study makes it important for the youth leader and the student to follow the chapter topics in succession, at least for the first time.

D e d i c a t i o n

The effort put into this book is dedicated to my parents, Tom and Judi Matlock. Their love was never ending, their discipline just, and their instruction wise. Without my parents I might never have come to know Jesus as my Savior and submit to His leading in my life.

Mom and Dad I thank you for living your lives as Ambassadors of Christ. Your living example of Godliness has cried out to me far more than words ever could have. I still look to your lives as guidance in my life now as a Husband and Father.

A book like this is
never the result of one man's work but
the influence of many lives directed by God's leading. I
would like to acknowledge much of the influence behind the completion of
this book, knowing that every effort was done not to get their names on this page, but so the
glory of the Lord would be made known.

Dawson McAllister whisked me away from my ministry path as an anthropological consultant on the mission field and gave me a vision for teaching serious content to students. Dawson has always grilled me and never let me rest on talent to get by. Dawson, thanks for teaching me to tango with good ol' Connie Content, and giving me a great opportunity to continue what you began for the Kingdom of God.

Al Macdonald raised the standard of excellence in my life and continues to do so. Al also let me experiment with doing the teaching journal in four colors at his expense.

The WisdomWorks Board of Directors, David DeYoung, Eric McHenry, David McDaniel, and Alf Laukoter who hold me accountable in my relationships with Christ, wife and children.

Jade Matlock, my gracious wife who saw the vision for this journal and conference even though it meant giving up precious time together. Jade is more than a wife – she is my "silent" partner in ministry. Without her blessing, permission and understanding I never would have written this.

Youth Pastor, Clark Barton gave me the inspiration for the topic as we discussed themes and teaching concepts for a summer camp with Anniston Road Baptist Church.

Greg Wilson, who met me for long discussions about the conference subject and teaching strategy even on the days just before his wedding. Greg also helped gather and compile many of the projects and statistics found in the journal.

Wayne Peterson tirelessly reviewed, edited, researched collateral material, and managed the production of this journal.

Russ Chilcoat and Shatrine Weik caught my vision for doing this journal in full color utilizing modern design techniques and blew me away with the layout. The late hours, frustrating deadlines and an overly demanding author didn't seem to exist for them as they Glorified God with their creativity.

A c k n o w l e d g e m e n t s

whoever claims to live in him must walk as Jesus did.

1 John 2.6

table of contents

Let's take a walk....

chapter 1

NOT OF THIS WORLD
being an ambassador for Christ

Have you realized how different you are from everybody else? No one is exactly like you, even if you are a twin! Your hair and skin color, height, weight, your personality — all these characteristics combine to make you one of a kind! When you visit friends you may realize that your family is different from other families. You may have noticed cultural differences too if you have moved to a different state or a different country. God created you to be different from the rest of the world.

Are We Really Different from the World? • As Christians, we are told by
God that we are to be different from the world in another way. We are to be like Christ. Why is this? Because we have been saved by Christ and the Holy Spirit is living in us! The Bible tells us that we have become new people. Notice what the Apostle Paul says:

2 Corinthians 5:17
Therefore, if anyone is in Christ, he is a new creation; the old has gone, the new has come!

Why is it then that lifestyles of Christians and non-Christians are so similar? When it comes to issues like premarital sex, divorce, cheating in school, partying, lying and stealing, the attitudes and behaviors of Christians are not very different from the world.

How Different Are We?

Apparently, the differences between the attitudes and behaviors of Christians and non-Christians are minimal. In a study of teenagers, pollster George Barna found that "born again" students were nearly as likely as other students to cheat on an exam, to steal possessions, to look through a pornographic magazine, or to have had sexual intercourse. Barna states, "apart from their engagement in religious activity, most teenagers' lives do not seem to have been substantially altered by their faith views." Here are Barna's findings: **>**

	Christians	Non-Christians
Volunteered Time to Help Needy People	49%	44%
Watched an X-rated or Pornographic Movie	32%	41%
Cheated on a test in school	29%	27%
Had sexual intercourse	23%	29%
Stolen from someone else	6%	7%
Looked through a pornographic magazine	5%	8%

Source: George Barna, Generation Next (Glendale, CA: Barna Research Group, 1995).

In another study, Barna found that during the past three months two out of every three (66%) church-attending students (ages 11-18) lied to a parent, teacher or other adult. Six in ten (59%) lied to their peers. One in three (36%) cheated on an exam. Nearly one in four (23%) smoked a cigarette or used another tobacco product. One in nine (12%) had gotten drunk. And nearly one in ten (8%) has used illegal drugs.
Source: George Barna, Baby Busters (Chicago: Northfield Publishing, 1992).

And yet God wants us to be different! In today's culture it is considered cool to be different and to be an individual. Would you believe that one of the most incredible ways you could be different is to be a true follower of Jesus Christ?!

If you are a Christian, how are your attitudes and behaviors different from your non-Christian friends?
....
....
....

Do you think a non-Christian would be able to identify you as a Christian by your behavior? ....
....

In this journal, we will try to understand how to think and see the world from God's perspective. You might be wearing a WWJD bracelet right now. Often we ask ourselves "What Would Jesus Do?," yet if we don't see life as Christ does, it is a very difficult question to answer. In the next several chapters we will learn that we are not of this world and by the time we finish, hopefully, our lives should prove it!

What is "The World"? • This is a very good question! Many people throw around the word, but very few stop to explain what it means.

What the World is Not

Not the Planet
When referring to "the world" in this journal, we will not be thinking of the planet earth itself. God created the earth and all that is in it. While the earth has been a victim of humanity and sin, the world expresses the very character of God.

Romans 1:20

For since the creation of the world God's invisible qualities — his eternal power and divine nature — have been clearly seen, being understood from what has been made, so that men are without excuse.

Not People

When referring to the world in this journal, it is not a reference to people. God loves people. Christ died for them. While there are sinful people in the world, they are not what we are trying to avoid in our lives. We have a responsibility to reach these people, not avoid or condemn them.

John 3:16

For God so loved the world that He gave His one and only Son, that whoever believes in Him shall not perish but have eternal life.

What "The World" DOES mean in this Book

A System of Belief

"The World" as used in this journal is a theological term used to describe the sinful system of our society as a whole. As we will learn, the world's system is based on principles of living that set themselves up against a Holy God.

Colossians 2:20

Since you died with Christ to the basic principles of this world, why, as though you still belonged to it, do you submit to its rules...?

03

Most humans follow the patterns of this system, which are dark and controlled by Satan. Christ died to set us free from this system so that in His power, we could "break out."

Colossians 1:13

For he has rescued us from the dominion of darkness and brought us into the kingdom of the Son he loves,

Words used for "World"

In the New Testament several words are used to define the "world." Here are some used in the Greek language to represent the English word "world."

Aion – meaning "an age," "a period of time." In the New Testament aion is translated "world" in the New International Version eight times. (Luke 16:8; Romans 12:2; 1 Corinthians 1:20; Ephesians 2:2, 6:12; 1 Timothy 6:17; 2 Timothy 4:10 ; Hebrews 9:26) • *Ephesians 6:12 For our struggle is not against flesh and blood, but against the rulers, against the authorities, against the powers of this dark world and against the spiritual forces of evil in the heavenly realms.*

Ge – comes from the word for soil, refers to regions, countries, or the earth as a whole, and is translated "the earth," "land," "ground." It occurs 250 times in the New Testament, but is translated "world" only six times in the New International Version. • *Rev 13:3 One of the heads of the beast seemed to have had a fatal wound, but the fatal wound had been healed. The whole world was astonished and followed the beast.*

Oikumene – comes from a root word meaning, "house", means "inhabited earth," and many times in Greek literature is a reference to the land or people of the Roman Empire. • *Luke 2:1 In those days Caesar Augustus*

>

ior high group. I stood on the edge of the pool and prayed, "I believe." Then I stepped off the edge, hoping to walk on the water just as Jesus and Peter did. I

issued a decree that a census should be taken of the entire Roman world.

Kosmos – meaning "order" or "arrangement." This is the most frequent Greek word that is translated "world" in English. Kosmos can have three meanings. The first is "all that is created." The second meaning is the "arena where human life and experience occur," and the third meaning is a reference to humanity itself. As a theological term, kosmos portrays human society as a system warped by sin, tormented by beliefs and desires and emotions that surge blindly and uncontrollably. The world system is a dark system operating on basic principles that are not of God. (Source: Expository Dictionary of Bible Words, Lawrence O. Richards, 1991 Zondervan Corporation).

• *Titus 2:12 It teaches us to say "No" to ungodliness and worldly (kosmos) passions, and to live self-controlled, upright and godly lives in this present age (aion),*

• *Matt 16:26 What good will it be for a man if he gains the whole world, yet forfeits his soul? Or what can a man give in exchange for his soul?*

Living Like An Alien • As believers in Christ, we are aliens and strangers in this world. An alien is someone who comes from one country to go to another. The ways of life may be unfamiliar to them. The language used to communicate is not the home language of the alien. Even clothing, food, and holidays are different.

1 Peter 2:11-12
Dear friends, I urge you as aliens and strangers in this world, to abstain from sinful desires, which war against your soul. Live such good lives among the pagans that, though they accuse you of doing wrong, they may see your good deeds and glorify God on the day he visits us.

As Christians we are in a place that is completely foreign to our true home (heaven). This world is simply a temporary place for us until we see Jesus again.

Philippians 3:20
But our citizenship is in heaven. And we eagerly await a Savior from there, the Lord Jesus Christ,

God desires to affect every part of our lives, if only we will let Him!

Romans 12:1-2
Therefore, I urge you, brothers, in view of God's mercy, to offer your bodies as living sacrifices, holy and pleasing to God —this is your spiritual act of worship.
Do not conform any longer to the pattern of this world, but be transformed by the renewing of your mind. Then you will be able to test and approve what God's will is — his good, pleasing and perfect will.

Conform: to fashion alike, i.e. conform oneself (in mind and character) to another's pattern; comes from the term from which we get the English word, "schematic."

Transform: to change into another form, literally or figuratively; comes from the term from which we get the English words, "metamorphosis,"and "morph."

Renew: a renewal, renovation, complete change for the better.

Because of all that God has done for us, we need to respond to Him. We are told to not conform to the pattern of the world, but to change the very way we think about life. The patterns of the world are like a computer program that is full of bugs. It seems to run okay for a while and then for no apparent reason, the whole system shuts down. God wants us to use His "operating system" for living our lives.

The transformation of our minds allows us to test and see what the will of God is. So many times we ask ourselves, "What is God's will for my life?" This verse tells us we will be able to know and approve of His will when we break out of the world's enslaving pattern of thinking and think as God designed us to think.

We are to be *in* the world, not *of* the world.

Four Ways Christians Act in this World •

The Secluded Christian

This person tries to avoid the world at all costs, never associating with it. He has no non-Christian friends; he reads only Christian books and listens to only Christian music. He is afraid of being influenced by the world and avoids it at all costs.

We must love the people of the world as Christ did. Jesus did not avoid the world at all. In fact, Jesus associated with sinners so much that the religious leaders condemned Him for His actions.

Matthew 11:19
The Son of Man came eating and drinking, and they say, "Here is a glutton and a drunkard, a friend of tax collectors and sinners.'" But wisdom is proved right by her actions.

Jesus showed love, not judgment, to sinners.

John 3:16
For God so loved the world that He gave His one and only Son, that whoever believes in Him shall not perish but have eternal life.

John 12:47-48
As for the person who hears my words but does not keep them, I do not judge him. For I did not come to judge the world, but to save it. There is a judge for the one who rejects me and does not accept my words; that very word which I spoke will condemn him at the last day.

What would it be like if Jesus had avoided the people of the world?

The Danger of being a Secluded Christian

While life may seem safe, the secluded Christian will miss opportunities to be used by God. It is God's desire that we reflect His love to a hurting world.

Matthew 5:13-16

"You are the salt of the earth. But if the salt loses its saltiness, how can it be made salty again? It is no longer good for anything, except to be thrown out and trampled by men. You are the light of the world. A city on a hill cannot be hidden. Neither do people light a lamp and put it under a bowl. Instead they put it on its stand, and it gives light to everyone in the house. In the same way, let your light shine before men, that they may see your good deeds and praise your Father in heaven."

He has placed us in the world to be salt and light, to give it flavor, and to show the way. We can only do this if we are involved, and not secluded.

The Legalistic Christian

Living the Christian life would be very simple if we only had a list of rules to determine everything that we do. Right?

Rules do tend to make everything clear, but Christ came to set us free and give us life. If we were bound to a bunch of rules, we would spend more time trying to understand the rules than doing what He intended for us.

Some Christians like to take the easy way out and become legalists. Rather than wrestling with their position in the world and with other Christians, they try to live according to rules and enjoy holding others to them.

Colossians 2:20-23

Since you died with Christ to the basic principles of this world, why, as though you still belonged to it, do you submit to its rules: "Do not handle! Do not taste! Do not touch!"? These are all destined to perish with use, because they are based on human commands and teachings. Such regulations indeed have an appearance of wisdom, with their self-imposed worship, their false sense of humility and their harsh treatment of the body, but they lack any value in restraining sensual indulgence.

In Paul's day many schools of thought existed regarding how a Christian should live. Often the easiest way to "set a standard" was to impose a rule like "Christians don't eat beef." While abstention from things of this life seems like significant change, Paul questioned the validity of most of it.

True Christians should not get bogged down trying to figure out what they can't do in life, but instead learn what God wants them to do. In order to do this, Christians must go beyond meager "rules" that, as Paul says, lack any value in restraining sensual indulgence. The true Christian seeks to glorify God in true worship, true wisdom, and true purpose in the world.

Some Black and White Issues

Now there are some very clear guidelines in Scripture about certain behavior. What are some of these? Consider the following verses, and write in the space given what God wants us to do or refrain from doing.

1 Thessalonians 4:3
It is God's will that you should be sanctified: that you should avoid sexual immorality;

God wants me to .... (Hint: "Sanctified" means to be different from the world by being cleansed by Christ and set apart for His service.)

God wants me to avoid ....

Ephesians 5:1-2
Be imitators of God, therefore, as dearly loved children and live a life of love, just as Christ loved us and gave himself up for us as a fragrant offering and sacrifice to God.

God wants me to .... and ....

Ephesians 5:3-4
But among you there must not be even a hint of sexual immorality, or of any kind of impurity, or of greed, because these are improper for God's holy people. Nor should there be obscenity, foolish talk or coarse joking, which are out of place, but rather thanksgiving.

God wants me to avoid even a hint of ...., or any kind of .... or ....; I am also to avoid ...., ..., and ....

Instead, God wants me to have an attitude of ....

Leviticus 19:11
Do not steal. Do not lie. Do not deceive one another.

God wants me to avoid ...., ..., and ....

Ephesians 6:1-3
Children, obey your parents in the Lord, for this is right. "Honor your father and mother"— which is the first commandment with a promise— "that it may go well with you and that you may enjoy long life on the earth."

God wants me to .... my parents.

What are some issues that are not as clear in the Word of God? ....
....
....

For example, does the Bible tell us about dating, and whom to date, and the limits we should have? How about things like dancing, smoking, and being a "meat-eater" vs being a vegetarian? Can you list other topics that are not clear from the Word?..
....
....
....

The Danger of being a Legalistic Christian

Most of the time legalistic Christians lose the joy of fellowship in their relationships because they are always holding everyone and themselves to "the rules." This causes fighting and a critical, negative attitude.

Many legalistic Christians have lost or never experienced the "joy" of their salvation because they are so caught up trying to keep the rules. In a sense they feel like they are working to keep or earn their salvation instead of enjoying salvation as the incredibly free gift Christ offers.

Isaiah 29:13
The Lord says: "These people come near to me with their mouth and honor me with their lips, but their hearts are far from me. Their worship of me is made up only of rules taught by men.

Galatians 5:1,13
It is for freedom that Christ has set us free. Stand firm, then, and do not let yourselves be burdened again by a yoke of slavery. 13. You, my brothers, were called to be free. But do not use your freedom to indulge the sinful nature; rather, serve one another in love.

The Worldly Christian

This person is out of balance in the world while trying to be a Christian. He has desired to be Christ-like, but can't give up his primary focus on things of this world. He is trying to save his life on earth and grab all the gusto it offers; but he will be frustrated and unhappy in his pursuits.

Matthew 16:25-26
For whoever wants to save his life will lose it, but whoever loses his life for me will find it. What good will it be for a man if he gains the whole world, yet forfeits his soul? Or what can a man give in exchange for his soul?

Colossians 2:8
See to it that no one takes you captive through hollow and deceptive philosophy, which depends on human tradition and the basic principles of this world rather than on Christ.

Colossians 3:1-2
Since, then, you have been raised with Christ, set your hearts on things above, where Christ is seated at the right hand of God. Set your minds on things above, not on earthly things.

The Danger of Being a Worldly Christian

While it may seem that the worldly Christian has lots of good times and friends, he will miss what it truly means to live for Christ. With a focus on earth, he completely forgets why God put us here. Christ died for us so that we could have a new life of service for Him. Christ wants us to join in on that new life which will bring eternal rewards.

Romans 6:1-4

What shall we say, then? Shall we go on sinning so that grace may increase? By no means! We died to sin; how can we live in it any longer? Or don't you know that all of us who were baptized into Christ Jesus were baptized into his death? We were therefore buried with him through baptism into death in order that, just as Christt was raised from the dead through the glory of the Father, we too may live a new life.

The Christian Ambassador

2 Corinthians 5:20

We are therefore Christ's ambassadors, as though God were making His appeal through us....

This person realizes that God has given him a place in this world to represent the Kingdom of Heaven. In love he seeks to advance the Kingdom of God by allowing Christ in his life to be an example to those around him. He looks at life completely different, because he does not represent himself or the world, but Jesus Christ.

What is an ambassador?

ambassador (am-bas-ə-dər) 1 a diplomatic official of the highest rank appointed to a foreign government as the resident representative of his own government or appointed for a special and often temporary diplomatic assignment 2 an authorized representative or messenger.

List some ways this definition of an ambassador can be characteristic also of the Christian life............
....
....
....

a) An ambassador is on a mission far from home

John 17:15-18

My prayer is not that you take them out of the world but that you protect them from the evil one. They are not of this world, even as I am not of it. Sanctify them by the truth; your word is truth. As you sent me into the world I have sent them into the world.

Ambassadors travel far from their true homes in order to represent the kingdom or country sending them. They are strangers in a foreign land. They have not left their homeland for a lifetime, but for a period of time in order to serve the country they represent. As Christians we are representatives of our true home, heaven. Under the authority of God and Christ we have been sent to serve.

b) An ambassador must die to himself

Philippians 1:21
For to me, to live is Christ and to die is gain.

Matthew 16:24-25
Then Jesus said to his disciples, "If anyone would come after me, he must deny himself and take up his cross and follow me. For whoever wants to save his life will lose it, but whoever loses his life for me will find it.

When a person is an ambassador he does not represent himself, but the kingdom that sent him. The way he dresses and the manner in which he conducts himself must be done in such a way to best represent the kingdom he serves. In a sense, the ambassador must die to his own wishes, and his desire is to serve his homeland. When in another country, the ambassador is there for purposes other than his own and must submit to the governing authorities in his homeland.

c) A Christian Ambassador glorifies God in every part of his life

1 Corinthians 10:31
"So whether you eat or drink or whatever you do, do it all to the glory of God."

In order to serve the kingdom in the best possible way, the ambassador wants everyone to know who he represents. He may demonstrate his foreign culture in the way he speaks, the flags or emblems he wears and displays, the food he eats or customs the ambassador practices. The bottom line is the ambassador makes his homeland known to all. The ambassador also represents and makes known the directives of the governing authority of his homeland. As Ambassadors of Christ, we should strive to make God's ways and His character known in all we do.

The Danger of Being an Ambassador

An ambassador may be hated and despised by this world (and by the Secluded, Legalistic, and Worldly Christian as well).

John 15:18-19
If the world hates you, keep in mind that it hated me first. If you belonged to the world, it would love you as its own. As it is, you do not belong to the world, but I have chosen you out of the world. That is why the world hates you.

Why do you think the Christian Ambassador might face opposition from the people in the world? ....
....
....

Why do you think the Christian Ambassador might be ridiculed by the Secluded and Worldly Christian?
....
....
....

Three Aspects of the Christian Ambassador's Life •

In Worship

In order to worship, there must be an object of worship. You have heard people say things like, "he worships his car." The car would be the object of worship.

As Christians, our object of worship is the Trinity: God the Father, Jesus Christ the Son, and The Holy Spirit our helper.

What are some things the world worships? ....
....
....

What are some of the things that are very important to you, that God might even say you "worship"?
....
....

In Wisdom

The word "wisdom" basically means "seeing how to live life." Wisdom is a perspective on how to live. As Christians, our source of wisdom is the Bible, God's very own Word. Only God's Word can give us the right perspective for living life.

The world trusts in all kinds of empty philosophies and forms of wisdom.

What are some examples of the wisdom of the world? ....
....
....

In Mission

As followers of Christ we realize that God has a plan and purpose for our lives. We are not to waste time doing foolish things, but we are to be God's representatives on this earth.

The world is full of hopelessness because it has no plan or purpose.

What are some reasons the world has for living? ....
....
....

What are some reasons God has us here? ....
....
....
....

Becoming Aware of Worldly Patterns • It is interesting to note that the world calls Christians "closed-minded" and unoriginal. So many people in this life believe that they are free to make their own choices and to think as they wish. This is a deception that comes from not having God's truth about life. God says that there is a pattern to the world's thinking. A pattern is a repetitious design that repeats itself again and again! The world has the conformity problem — not Christians. We are to transform every part of our life.

PROJECT: Identifying the World's Patterns

We can see the patterns of this world more clearly when we break life down into various parts. Notice in the following list that there is nothing inherently wrong with any of these "areas" of life. It is how the world addresses these areas that give us insight into worldly patterns of living.

What are some of the world's patterns of belief in the following areas of life? Write down words or phrases that describe how you see the world addressing each of these areas.

Sex. ....

....

Music ....

....

Time ....

....

Money ....

....

Purpose in life ....

....

Choices ....

....

Clothing ....

....

Origins of the universe ....

....

When life begins ....

....

How do these patterns differ from the way God addresses these patterns in the Bible? ....

....

....

Conclusion • Which of the four types of Christians would you consider yourself to be? Secluded, Legalistic, Worldly, or Ambassador? ....

Which would you like to be? ....

At some point in our lives we must decide whether we are going to follow God or the world. As Christians we are told to be different because we are different. In the next chapters we will learn how to judge patterns from God's perspective, and then break down specific patterns of this world.

notes

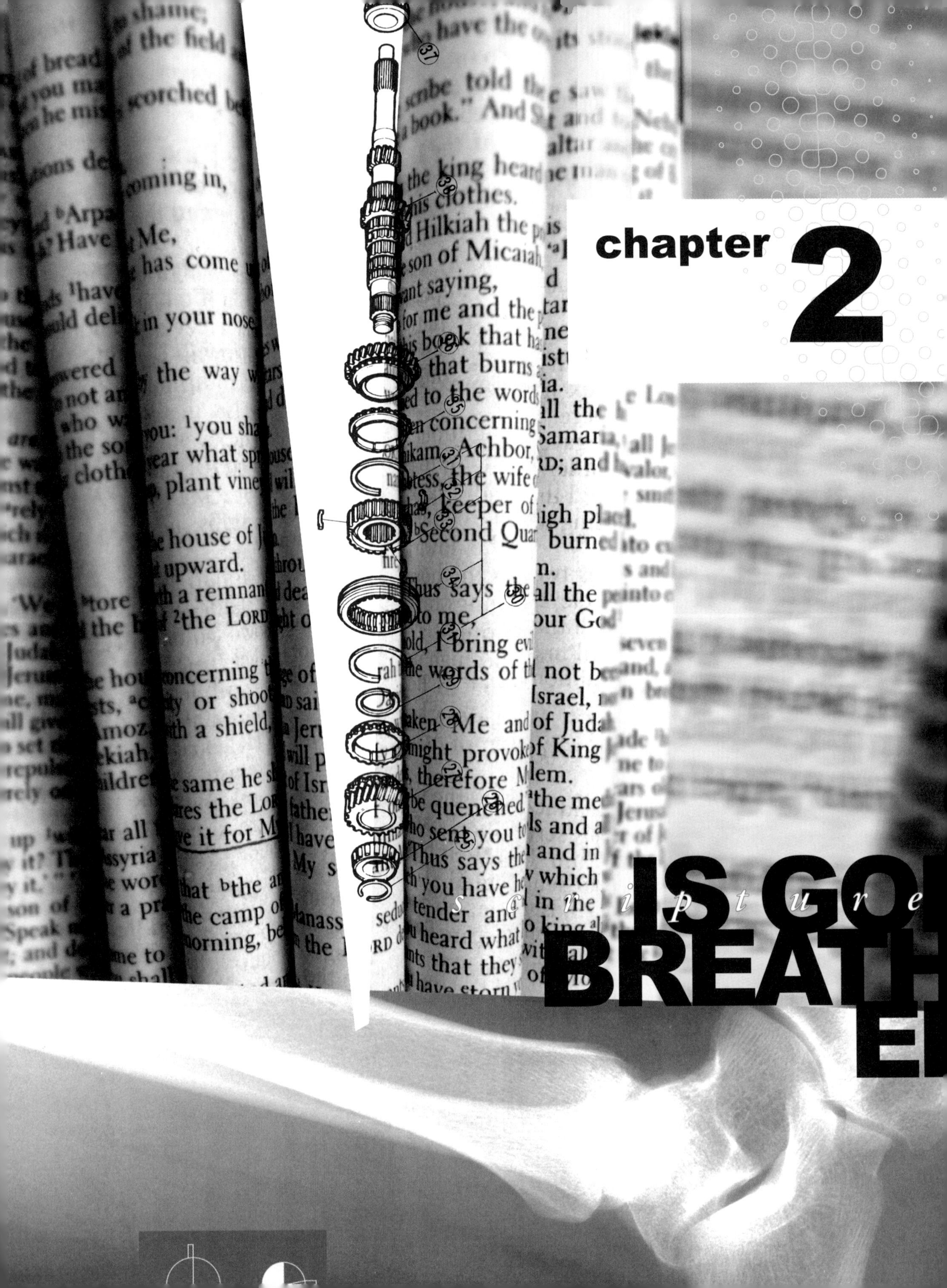

chapter 2

scripture IS GO
BREATH
E

GOD'S WORD
the standard by which we judge all patterns

Instead of conforming to the patterns of the world system, God wants us to be transformed. We are transformed by changing the way we think about God and the world around us.

Romans 12:2
Do not conform any longer to the pattern of this world, but be transformed by the renewing of your mind. Then you will be able to test and approve what God's will is – his good, pleasing and perfect will.

The Greek word for transform, from which we get the word "metamorphosis," means to change from one form to another. The change is just like the special effect of "morphing" used in movies to change one person into another, or a person into an animal. God wants to "morph" our lives into one that is like Christ's.

In order to "morph," one form must change to another. The first form is our life and our lifestyle as it is right now. The form we are changing to is Christ. If we are to become effective Ambassadors for Christ, and truly transform our thinking, then we must begin with God's Word. By reading the Bible we learn about Christ and His desired changes for us. God begins the change in us by giving us salvation. We then grow as Christians by studying the Bible and putting it into action in our lives.

Before we consider the changes for our lives in the chapters to come, it might be a good idea to check out our attitude toward God's Word.

Self-Check: My Attitude Toward God's Word •

Would you agree or disagree with the following statements? (circle your answer)

The Bible is the most important book ever written.	agree	disagree
The Bible is God's Word.	agree	disagree
The Bible has answers to all of life's questions.	agree	disagree

You probably agreed to most of the above statements (they are all true). Now answer this question: How many minutes last week did you spend reading the most important book ever written? ....

Chances are, you haven't spent much time reading God's Word. Why not? ....
....
....

If the Bible is such an important book, and it does so much for our lives, why don't we read it more often?
....
....
....

This chapter will explore how to properly think about the Bible, God's Word.

The Bible Is Our Operation Manual While on this Earth •

John 17:15-18
My prayer is not that you take them out of the world but that you protect them from the evil one. They are not of this world, even as I am not of it. Sanctify them by the truth; your word is truth. As you sent me into the world I have sent them into the world.

Jesus Christ is praying to God that we would be sanctified by the truth. The word "sanctified" means "cleansed and set apart for service." Many people want to be set apart to be used of God, yet many overlook that they must be cleansed first. Your mother may have China plates that are used only for the best occasions. In a sense, those plates have been "set apart" for special service. What good would it be if she never washed them? How special could they possibly be? The truth not only sets us apart for special use, but also cleanses us for that purpose.

Jesus then goes on to say that God's Word is truth. If we are going to be safe in this world and accomplish God's plan for us, we must follow God's truth, the Bible.

God's Word Keeps Us Pure

Psalm 119:9
"How can a young man keep his way pure? By living according to your word."

God wants us to know that His Word will protect us from an impure life. The Bible is a light to us when we don't know what to do.

Here is a wonderful perspective from one who has a good attitude toward God's Word. Just imagine the joy and excitement of the writer as you read the following passage.

Psalm 119:97-100
"Oh, how I love your law! I meditate on it all day long. Your commands make me wiser than my enemies, for they are ever with me. I have more insight than my teachers, for I meditate on your statutes. I have more understanding than the elders, for I obey your precepts."

God's Word Protects Us From Our Enemies

God's Word will protect you from harm. Our foremost enemy is Satan, the devil. We know that God's Word keeps us safe from the devil by showing us the truth and leading us to salvation.

How has God's Word protected you from harm? Have you ever decided not to give into a temptation that could have harmed you because of a specific promise or command in Scripture? Explain. ....

....

....

....

17

God's Word Gives Us Tremendous Insight

The Bible is the source of all true knowledge. Many teachers know facts, but they do not see this information in its true context. The Bible reveals not only truth, but truth in action. In the last chapter we called this wisdom. Many teachers know truth, but few are wise.

Scripture teaches us about the character and nature of God, about ourselves and others, and about the world around us. What are some things that you have learned from the Bible? ....

....

....

God's Word Gives Us Understanding Beyond Our Years

An "elder" is an older person who has had time to gain wisdom through experience. For instance, you learn to not touch a burning coal with your hand, because you have either been burned, or have seen others burn their hands. This experience leads to understanding that keeps you from being burned.

God's Word gives us a jump-start on life, by giving us wisdom well beyond our years. God shows us in advance how life works. How has knowing God's Word helped you avoid the pressures and temptations that other teenagers face? Are there other struggles you could have avoided by taking to heart the wisdom in God's Word? Explain. ....
....
....
....

Proper Attitudes Towards God's Word •

Proverbs 2: 1-5

"My son, if you accept my words and store up my commands within you, turning your ear to wisdom and applying your heart to understanding, and if you call out for insight and cry aloud for understanding, and if you look for it as for silver and search for it as for hidden treasure, then you will understand the fear of the Lord and find the knowledge of God."

Let's look at each attitude mentioned in Proverbs 2:1-5

Accept God's Words

Before you can get anything out of God's Word, you have to be willing to accept the truth in it. This means that you will say to God, "If you say it, I'll believe it!" And part of accepting the truth is being willing to put it into practice in your life, whether you want to or not.

Is the Bible True?

If the Bible isn't the Word of God, then why study it? If it is simply a collection of human wisdom, then it is no more helpful to you than studying any of the other man-made philosophies that line the shelves of any bookstore. Let's start with what the Bible says about itself. 2 Timothy 3:16 says that "all Scripture is God-breathed."

• 2 Timothy 3:16 All Scripture is God-breathed and is useful for teaching, rebuking, correcting and training in righteousness

That basically means that every word of Scripture is straight from the mouth of God. 2 Peter 1:21 says that although the words of Scripture were written by men, those men "spoke from God as they were carried along by the Holy Spirit."

• 2 Peter 1:21 For prophecy never had its origin in the will of man, but men spoke from God as they were carried along by the Holy Spirit.

>

Clearly, Scripture teaches us that the Bible is the very Word of God. So, either Scripture is wrong (or lying) about its own nature, or it really is the Word of God. If Scripture isn't really the true Word of God, then 2 Timothy 3:16 and 2 Peter 1:21 are not true. If one part of Scripture can't be trusted, can any of it be trusted? Either all of the Bible is true, or none of it is true.

Store Up God's Commands Within You

Instead of storing God's knowledge in a book, you should store it in your life! This happens through the memorization of God's Word and obedience to God's commands.

Turn Your Ear Toward Wisdom

Have you ever wanted to listen in on a conversation you were not part of? If you have, you know that you want to hear as much as you can and so you "turn your ear" toward the conversation. God wants us to listen actively to His conversation with us. You turn your ear to wisdom when you show up for Bible studies and take time to read and discuss God's Word.

Apply Your Heart

Do you have a hobby, sport, or activity that you enjoy? If you do, then you understand what it means to apply your heart: you give it all you've got. The heart is the center place of our lives. To understand God's Word we have to be passionate about getting it into our lives. That inner motivation must be there.

Call Out For Insight

Trying to understand God's Word can sometimes be frustrating. Much like solving word problems in math, you can get so frustrated you just want to scream. It is with that intensity that we should study God's Word. We should want to know it so much, that when it seems unclear, we would call out to another Christian who could help us understand (like a parent, pastor, or youth pastor). We also need to be willing to cry out to God for help in understanding His Word.

Search For Truth As If It Were Hidden Treasure

Did you ever lose something in your bedroom or house that you really needed? Immediately you went into a frenzy going through drawers and turning over every inch of the house until you found what you were looking for.

We should have that same attitude of searching in God's Word. We are digging for buried treasure that will be ours to keep and will change our lives forever. God's Word is like a gold mine: we must dig to find hidden treasure to make it applicable to our lives.

Be Ready To Do Something • When we dig into God's Word, we must be ready to do what we learn.

James 1:22
"Do not merely listen to the word, and so deceive yourselves. Do what it says."

God's Word is clear. Many hear, but few do anything about it. When we spend time in church or in Bible study and do not change, we are deceiving ourselves. So many people believe that the simple act of going to church and hearing the pastor preach is all they need. God says they are deceiving themselves.

James 1:23, 24
"Anyone who listens to the word but does not do what it says is like a man who looks at his face in a mirror and, after looking at himself, goes away and immediately forgets what he looks like."

Imagine! You wake up in the morning and go to the mirror. Upon examination of your face, you notice that you have a bright green booger hanging out of your nose. Do you think you would forget about such a thing and go to school? NO WAY!

You would take care of the neon green snot immediately. James tells us that reading God's Word is like looking in a mirror. If we see something that needs to be addressed in our lives, we should take care of it immediately!

James 1:25
"But the man who looks intently into the perfect law that gives freedom, and continues to do this, not forgetting what he has heard, but doing it — he will be blessed in what he does."

Let's face it – talk is cheap. One of the most disappointing experiences in life is when a person says one thing and does another. It grieves a teacher when he teaches a student correctly but then the student does not apply it to his life. God wants us to come to the Word ready to act because it confronts the very way we live. We must be more than hearers, we must be doers!

PROJECT: How to Study the Bible (and Actually Learn Something)
The Bible speaks to the issues that you face every day: your faith, your family, your friends, your education, your job, your attitude and your health. The Bible is not boring. It is God's personal Word to you and it explains everything you need to know to live successfully as God's ambassador in this world. But in order to benefit from its wisdom you need to study what it says so that you can understand it. There are many different English translations of the Bible. It is best to read from a more contemporary translation that is easier to understand. Some good contemporary translations are: New International Version, Contemporary English Version, New Living Translation, and The Message. If you don't have a contemporary translation, ask your parents or your youth leader to help you find one.

Once you have a contemporary version of Scripture in your hand, there are several different approaches you can take to studying it. Here are three approaches to help you get started. Ask your youth pastor for some other ideas.

1. You can take a book from the Bible that looks interesting and read it from start to finish. Ask God to help you see why He included that book in Scripture and what value it has for your life.

2. Take a personality from the Bible (like Ruth or David) and read everything you can about that person. Read about how that person walked (or failed to walk) with God and look for examples of behaviors and attitudes to follow or to avoid.

3. Try using a topical study method. That is what you are doing with this manual—studying what the Bible says about worldly patterns of behavior. Take an issue that is important to you and read what God has to say about that particular issue. You can do a topical study right now using the chart titled "What the Bible Says About..." Pick a topic from the chart and look up the verses that apply to that topic.

When you read a passage from the Bible, be sure to look at the whole context of that passage—who is speaking, to whom they are speaking, what point they are trying to make, etc. Then ask yourself how you can apply that passage to your life. How is the passage relevant to your life right now? Look for a verse to memorize, a promise to believe, a command to obey, a principle to apply, a sin to confess, or a personal example to follow.

What the Bible Says About...

...how to become a Christian - John 1:12, 3:16-18 and 5:24, Acts 4:12, Romans 3:23, 6:23 and 5:8, 1 Peter 3:18
...how to know for sure you are going to heaven - John 3:36 and 5:24, 1 John 5:11-13
...God's forgiveness - Psalm 103:12, Ephesians 1:7, 1 John 1:9
...forgiving others - Matthew 6:14-15, Ephesians 4:32
...you - Psalm 139, Jeremiah 29:11
...your responsibilities to your parents - Proverbs 1:8, 10:1, 13:1 and 23:22, Ephesians 6:1-3, Colossians 3:20
...your parents' responsibilities to you - Deuteronomy 6:6-9, Proverbs 22:6 and 29:17, Ephesians 6:4
...love and dating -   Proverbs 4:23, 1 Corinthians 13:4-7, 2 Corinthians 6:14
...sex - Genesis 2:24, 1 Corinthians 6:18, 1 Thessalonians 4:3, Hebrews 13:4
...hanging out with the "wrong crowd" - Proverbs 24:1-2, 1 Corinthians 15:33
...grieving the death of a loved one - John 11:25-26 and 14:1-4
...how to know right from wrong (find the four Biblical principles in) - 1 Corinthians 6:12, 8:9, 10:23 and 10:31
...what God's will is for you - 1 Thessalonians 4:3, and 5:16-18, 1 Timothy 2:3-4, 1 Peter 2:15
...dealing with temptation - Matthew 26:41, 1 Corinthians 10:13, Hebrews 2:18 and 4:15
...the world - Matthew 5:14 and 16:26, John 3:16, 16:33 and 18:36, James 4:4, 1 John 2:15-17

21

Time to Commit • For the next two weeks I will spend at least 5-10 minutes a day reading God's Word. If while reading, I learn something that requires action, I will not only hear, but I will do what it tells me.

Student: ....

Adult (parent/youth pastor/sponsor): ....

Date: ....

chapter 3

PARTY
GIRLS
FUN

LIQUOR
BEER & WINE

SATURDAYS
SESSION
ATE
NIGHT STARTS WEEK NO
830
730

Pulmonary Artery

Vena
Cava

Aorta

L. Atrium

Pulmonary
Veins

L. Auricle

R. Auricle

Coronary
Vessels

R. Atrium

L. Ventricle

ENSLAVED BY
ALL KINDS OF

PAS-
SIONS & pleasures

PATTERNS OF PLEASURE

In the previous chapter, we made a commitment that we would spend at least 5-10 minutes a day reading God's Word. And if while reading, we learned something that required action, we would not only hear, but would do what God told us. We have an opportunity now to put that into practice, as we consider the Patterns of Pleasure. In this chapter we will examine the motives behind actions in our life. While motives are often hard to determine, we will try to zero in on the object of pleasure. Are you living to please yourself, to please others, or to please God?

Proverbs 21:17
He who loves pleasure will become poor...

What is Pleasure? • Pleasure can simply be defined as that which is pleasing. But pleasing to whom? What pleases one person may not be pleasing to another.

Think through the list below. Describe how each item could be good, or could be detrimental to you as a Christian.

Music styles ....

Food ....

Clothing ....

Vehicle choices ....

Hobbies ....

Sexual Preferences ....

Sporting Activities ....

In what way should you, as an Ambassador of Christ in the world, pursue pleasure? As a Christian, God does want you to enjoy life. In fact, joy is one aspect of the fruit of the Spirit. Real joy however, is not found in doing what is pleasing to you, but in doing what is pleasing to God.

What are Worldly Patterns of Pleasure? • The Bible tells us that there are certain patterns of the world that we must avoid if we are to be ambassadors for Christ. These patterns are summarized in 1 John 2:15-17.

1 John 2:15-17
Do not love the world or anything in the world. If anyone loves the world, the love of the Father is not in him. For everything in the world — the cravings of sinful man, the lust of his eyes and the boasting of what he has and does — comes not from the Father but from the world. The world and its desires pass away, but the man who does the will of God lives forever.

John sees the worldy patterns as:
1. The Patterns of Pleasure ("the cravings of sinful man")
2. The Patterns of Possessions ("the lust of his eyes")
3. The Patterns of Position ("the boasting of what he has and does")
4. The Patterns of Purpose ("the man who does the will of God lives forever")

Becoming Enslaved to Your Cravings

The first of these patterns is pleasure. The Bible tells us that the world has an appetite for pleasure that does not come from God.

...For everything in the world — the cravings of sinful man, the lust of his eyes and the boasting of what he has and does ...

What does the Bible mean by "the cravings of sinful man"? In the days of the New Testament writers the concept of doing what was pleasing to the body was referred to as "hedonism." The focus of hedonism was to satisfy the desires of the body.

What are the desires of the body?

> Food — gluttony
>
> Sleep — laziness, slothfulness
>
> Elimination of pain — drugs, substance abuse
>
> Immediate (easy) gratification — theft, gambling, cheating
>
> Sexual fulfillment — premarital sex, homosexuality, inappropriate acts of affection (heavy petting, sensuality)
>
> Escape from reality — music, entertainment, video games
>
> Preservation of self — fighting, gossip, backstabbing, cheating, independence from authorities

Man's desire to do what is pleasing to himself, as opposed to what is pleasing to God, has been evident since the beginning of mankind. In the Garden of Eden, God had given man the right to eat any fruit from any tree with the exception of one. When Satan tempted Eve he appealed to her sense of pleasure. Would she please God or rather please her own appetite?

Genesis 3:6
When the woman saw that the fruit of the tree was good for food she took some and ate it....

To this very day we wrestle with the temptation to please ourselves rather than please God. The temptations have become more numerous. For Adam and Eve there was only one action that was displeasing to God, and that was the simple act of eating fruit from a forbidden tree. In our modern world the options for satisfying our own pleasure are too numerous to count.

Galatians 5:19-21
The acts of the sinful nature are obvious: sexual immorality, impurity and debauchery; idolatry and witchcraft; hatred, discord, jealousy, fits of rage, selfish ambition, dissensions, factions, and envy; drunkenness, orgies, and the like....

Acts of Sinful Nature

"Sexual immorality" refers to any sexual act between two people who are not married. It also refers to pornography, such as sexually explicit magazines and movies. *"Impurity"* refers to an immoral or unethical lifestyle. *"Debauchery"* refers to partying, abusing drugs and other lifestyles that recklessly disregard what is right. *"Idolatry"* is worshiping things that God has created instead of worshiping God. *"Witchcraft"* is tampering with evil, such as playing with Ouija boards and certain role-playing and card games that involve magic and spells. *"Hatred, discord, jealousy, fits of rage, selfish ambition, dissensions, factions and envy"* all refer to ways that we mistreat others. *"Drunkenness"* obviously refers to the sin of getting drunk, but also includes being under the influence of any mind-altering drug. *"Orgies"* refers to a wild, anything-goes lifestyle, primarily of a sexual nature. By adding *"and the like"* to the end of his list, Paul is saying that this list does not include all the ways that we try to satisfy our own cravings. Can you think of some other ways? ....
....
....

25

Finding Freedom from the Slavery

Titus 3:3-5
At one time we too were foolish and disobedient, deceived and enslaved by all kinds of passions and pleasures .... But when the kindness and love of God our Savior appeared, he saved us, not because of the righteous things we had done, but because of his mercy....

Before we were Christians, God's Word tells us we were slaves to passion and pleasure. If you had trusted Christ at an early age or are still young, you may never have fully experienced this type of slavery.

People's actions are influenced greatly by their inner desires. But life in Christ sets us free!

Even in secular twelve-step recovery programs you cannot escape addiction or compulsion (two forms of slavery to pleasure) without acknowledging a "higher power." If you trusted Christ at an early age, thank God that He saved you from experiencing a life enslaved to pleasure.

God's Perspective on Pleasure • Matthew tells us about Satan's temptation of Christ. Like Eve and all mankind, Christ was tempted to please himself. Unlike many, Christ overcame this. We will look to Christ as an example of how we can overcome this temptation.

Matthew 4:1-3
Then Jesus was led by the Spirit into the desert to be tempted by the devil. After fasting forty days and forty nights, he was hungry. The tempter came to him and said, "If you are the Son of God, tell these stones to become bread."

Satan had Jesus just where he wanted Him. Jesus hadn't eaten for forty days and nights! The Bible says it best: He was hungry! The human body of Christ was craving nourishment. Satan's request was simply for Jesus to provide for his need.

Why was this a temptation? ....
....

Remember, Jesus came to earth to die for our sin, and to show us how to live. Yes, Jesus was God, yet He humbled himself to become a man to show us how to live. Because of this Jesus chose not to use His Godly power. Instead He set it aside to live as a man completely dependent on the father.

Philippians 2:5-7
Your attitude should be the same as that of Christ Jesus: Who being in very nature God, did not consider equality with God something to be grasped, but made himself nothing, taking the very nature of a servant, being made in human likeness.

Jesus' feelings, cravings, and desires were real. To use his power as God to create food would have been a misuse of his attributes. He did not give in to his desire so that we might learn by his example how to defeat the temptation to satisfy our own needs.

Matthew 4:4
Jesus answered, "It is written: 'Man does not live on bread alone, but on every word that comes from the mouth of God.'"

Jesus was quoting Scripture (Deuteronomy 8:3) in his fight against temptation. His response to Satan was simply this: "Man does not live by fulfilling his desires, but from depending on God to meet his desires."

From Christ's example we learn that Christians should respond to pleasure by:

Living According to the Word of God

An ambassador acts according to the instruction and authority of the country he represents. As a Christian you should live according to the instruction given in the Word of God.

Jesus did not just believe the Scriptures to be a book of "really nice thoughts," but realized Scripture as an authority in His life. Christians must rely on God's Word for their guidance.

Depending on God, instead of Depending on Self

An ambassador relies completely on the kingdom that represents him to provide his needs. As a follower of Christ you should depend on God to meet your needs rather than relying on your own abilities to satisfy them.

What are some ways you have gotten in trouble by trying to meet your own needs? ....
....
....
....

PROJECT: Satisfying Our Own Needs

Below are some ways people attempt to meet their own needs instead of relying on God to satisfy them. Can you identify the need being met by each?

Alcohol/Drug abuse – *Need being met:* ....
....

Eating Disorders – *Need being met:* ....
....

Stealing – *Need being met:* ....
....

Lying – *Need being met:* ....
....

Cheating – *Need being met:* ....
....

Witchcraft – *Need being met:* ....
....

Gambling – *Need being met:* ....
....

Doing what Pleases God instead what Pleases Self

An ambassador does not act on what pleases him, but rather what pleases the kingdom he represents. As a follower of Christ you should seek to fill your life with those things that are pleasing to God.

Psalm 37:4
Delight yourself in the Lord and He will give you the desires of your heart.

So often we focus on the second part of this verse, namely, getting what we want. This verse seems encouraging, but it is difficult to do. How can we delight in the Lord?

What is Pleasing to God? •

Demonstrating the Fruit of the Spirit

In a letter to the Church in Galatia, the apostle Paul wrote about the evidence of God's presence. Right after his list of the acts of the sinful nature in verses 19-21, Paul lists qualities that God gives to his ambassadors. He called these qualities the fruit of the Spirit.

Galatians 5:22-25
But the fruit of the Spirit is love, joy, peace, patience, kindness, goodness, faithfulness, gentleness and self control. Against such things there is no law. Those who belong to Christ Jesus have crucified the sinful nature with its passions and desires. Since we live by the Spirit, let us keep in step with the Spirit.

Making Known the Character of God

Jeremiah 9:24
But let him who boasts boast about this: that he understands and knows me, that I am the Lord, who exercises kindness, justice and righteousness on earth, for in these I delight, declares the Lord.

God delights in those who boast about Him. Notice that you aren't supposed to hide that you know God, but are to boast about it. It seems then, that in everything you do, you should be making God known!

How can you make God known in your life? ....
....
....
....

God tells us that He exercises kindness, justice and righteousness. The activities then that please God are those that exhibit these characteristics.

SEX: Pursuing Pleasure from Sex with Whoever and Whenever

The world has placed a very casual nature on the sexual relationship. By removing sex and other sexually stimulating activities from the God-given context of a marriage relationship, the world has lost the true pleasure of sex that God intended.

God is pro-sex

In fact, sex is God's idea. God created sex for two reasons. First, God created sex as a means for a husband and wife to reproduce.

Genesis 1:27-28a
So God created man in his own image, in the image of God he created him; male and female he created them. God blessed them and said to them, "Be fruitful and increase in number; fill the earth and subdue it...."

God also created sex for pleasure between a husband and his wife; and only between a husband and his wife.

Proverbs 5:18-21
May your fountain be blessed, and may you rejoice in the wife of your youth. A loving doe, a graceful deer—may her breasts satisfy you always, may you ever be captivated by her love. Why be captivated, my son, by an adulteress? Why embrace the bosom of another man's wife? For a man's ways are in full view of the Lord, and he examines all his paths.

God intended sex for the marriage relationship

The Bible makes it clear that any sexual activity outside of a marriage relationship is against God's will.

1 Thessalonians 4:3-5
It is God's will that you should be sanctified: that you should avoid sexual immorality; that each of you should learn to control his own body in a way that is holy and honorable, not in passionate lust like the heathen, who do not know God.

"Sexual immorality" refers to any sexual activity outside of marriage, not just sexual intercourse. What are some other activities, which lead to sexual intercourse, and therefore should be reserved for marriage?....

....

....

The world says, "Go ahead and have sex with whomever you want." God says, "control your passions and save sex for your wedding night."

God does not want us seeking "temporary" sexual pleasure outside of the marriage relationship

Teenagers are physically capable and ready to have sex; but are not emotionally ready for the responsibilities of marriage and family. That's why so many teenagers have sex before they are married. Many teenage girls get pregnant every year; while many other teenagers contract sexually transmitted diseases as a result of not following God's plan for sex.

Proverbs 4:23
Above all else, guard your heart, for it is the wellspring of life.

Why do you think God designed you to be physically ready for sex before you are emotionally ready for marriage and a family? Does that seem unfair to you? Why or why not? ....
....
....
....

DRUGS: Pursuing Pleasure from Mind-Altering Substances

God has created our minds to work in amazing ways: He has given man incredible minds to think and make judgments. When we try to escape reality by short-circuiting the mind or impairing judgment we misuse the bodies God has given to us. Many drugs exist that have medicinal value (the Bible even speaks of the medicinal value of alcohol), but we are not to abuse substances for our pleasure.

It is interesting that many people think that drugs stimulate creativity, yet God who is the ultimate Creator (He made the world, you know) offers us a relationship with Him in which we can be co-creators with Him! Simply put, God wants us to depend on Him, not some substance, for our needs.

Our bodies are temples of the Holy Spirit purchased with a price

Have you ever heard or said, "It is my body and I will do what I want with it." For the Christian, that is not true. Jesus paid for your body when He died on the cross. It belongs to God and it has a new tenant, the Holy Spirit.

1 Corinthians 6:19-20
Do you not know that your body is a temple of the Holy Spirit, who is in you, whom you have received from God? You are not your own; you were bought at a price. Therefore, honor God with your body.

Drugs are a form of idolatry

Drugs can be either physically or psychologically addictive, or both. Unless taken under the supervision of a doctor for medical purposes, drugs will become your master. Christians are to have only one master—God.

1 Corinthians 6:12b
...“Everything is permissible for me”—but I will not be mastered by anything.

Do you know students who have allowed drugs or alcohol to become their master? ....
....

The Basketball Diaries

Jim Carroll is a poet, songwriter and musician whose autobiography, *The Basketball Diaries*, details his struggle with substance abuse during his teenage years. Between the ages of 12 and 16, Carroll spent his time playing basketball for his private school, writing poetry, and doing drugs on the streets of New York City with his friends. Although Carroll's talents for writing and basketball could have earned him a scholarship to a major university, he was instead kicked out of both his home and his private prep school because of his growing heroin addiction. Many students pay a high price for their addictions. What are some things that an addiction to drugs or alcohol could cost you?

....

....

Christ has delivered us from the slavery of passion and pleasure

Christ did all that was necessary to deliver us from slavery to drugs, alcohol and other passions and pleasures. In His death on the cross, He paid the price to redeem and deliver us.

Titus 3:3-5a
At one time we too were foolish, disobedient, deceived and enslaved by all kinds of passions and pleasures. We lived in malice and envy, being hated and hating one another. But when the kindness and love of God our Savior appeared, he saved us, not because of righteous things we had done, but because of his mercy...

ROCK-N-ROLL: Pursuing Pleasure from Entertainment and the Media

Entertainment has become a great source of pleasure abuse for students, particularly in the United States. Often it is not only the content alone that is displeasing to God, but also the time and money wasted on things that do not glorify Him.

The entertainment industry and the media are constantly bombarding us with messages. Many of those messages set themselves up against God and what we stand for as Christians. As ambassadors of Christ, we must not allow ourselves to be influenced by these messages.

2 Corinthians 10:5
We demolish arguments and every pretension that sets itself up against the knowledge of God, and we take captive every thought to make it obedient to Christ.

How do we do that? How can we live in the real world, with all of its mixed-up spiritual messages, and make every thought obedient to Christ? ....

....

....

....

Anyone who lives in the real world, who is committed to being salt and light as Christ's ambassador, will be exposed to these worldly influences. The key is not to let your mind dwell on those things. Instead, we must keep our minds focused on the things that matter to God.

Philippians 4:8
   Finally, brothers, whatever is true, whatever is noble, whatever is right, whatever is pure, whatever is lovely, whatever is admirable—if anything is excellent or praiseworthy—think about such things.

Estimate how much time you spend on entertainment. How much time do you think you spend in an average month on entertainment activities? ....

How much time to you spend with your family? ....

How much time do you spend with God? ....

Television Time

According to a 1990 survey by Newsweek, teenagers spend an average of twenty-two hours a week watching television. ("Teens and TV," Newsweek Special Issue, summer/fall 1990, 36). How does your television watching compare to the average teenager? Do you think 22 hours a week is too much television? Why or why not? ....
....
....
....

Estimate how much money you spend on entertainment. How much money do you think you spend on entertainment in a month? ....

How are you entertained? ....
....
....

In our society we are constantly given opportunities to please our senses with many types of media. Can you add to this list of the media elements in society?

Music
Television
Books
Movies
Videos
Internet
Magazines
Wall Art (paintings, poster, bumper stickers)
....
....
....
....
....

And what about the messages found in entertainment? Let's face it. Most of the entertainment we engage ourselves in pleases us more than it pleases God.

PROJECT: Mixed Messages

What are some of the messages found in the music, movies, video games, and television you watch? Listed below are some of the messages sent by the media, reflecting the worldly patterns of pleasure. Can you give a biblical response to each one?

	The Media Says...	God Says...
Violence	*entertaining*	....
Politics	*what's in it for me*	....
Physical appearance	*is very important*	....
Money/Materialism	*take all you can get*	....
Sex	*recreational/do it now*	....
Drugs	*relaxing, an escape from pain*	....

Realize there is no specific list of movies or music that God says you should or shouldn't see or listen to. God wants you to be constantly evaluating what you spend your time doing. Evaluate the messages against the filter of Philippians 4:8 and other principles from God's Word. Learn to love what God loves and hate what God hates.

Jesus said, "Man lives not on bread alone, but on the Word of God (Matthew 4:4). Are you living off the messages of entertainers or the Word of God?

33

Conclusion • One of the strongest worldly patterns is the desire to do what pleases ourselves. The world does whatever it finds pleasure in, even if it ends in emptiness and despair. Christ died so that we could find real pleasure in life. True pleasure comes from pleasing God and not ourselves.

The Bible says that in the end times, people will be "lovers of pleasure rather than lovers of God" (2 Timothy 3:4).

As ambassadors of the Kingdom of Heaven, we do what pleases God and not what pleases ourselves. When we do this, we find true satisfaction, and others come to know the One who is the source of all that is good and pleasing, Jesus Christ.

notes:

chapter **4**

CAST BUT a GLANCE

atriches
&theyaregon

PATTERNS OF POSSESSIONS

In the last chapter we looked at the Patterns of Pleasure in the world. We saw that the world's answer for pleasure is not lasting. As we continue to explore the passage in 1 John we learn of other worldly approaches to life.

1 John 2:15-17
Do not love the world or anything in the world. If anyone loves the world, the love of the Father is not in him. For everything in the world – the craving of sinful man, the lust of his eyes and the boasting of what he has and does – comes not from the Father but from the world. The world and its desires pass away, but the man who does the will of God lives forever.

What is "The Lust of The Eyes?" • This is a term basically describing our desire for things. The particular lust described here is one of coveting. While shopping, you see an item that you just gotta have. You can't get it out of your mind; you'll do just about anything to get it. That would be the lust of the eyes.

Satan appealed to Eve's lust of the eyes in the Garden of Eden. The fruit from the forbidden tree was the only thing she thought she had to have.

Genesis 3:6
When the woman saw that the fruit of the tree was good for food and pleasing to the eye she took some and ate it....

Can you relate to Eve's desire for something that was forbidden? Why do you think we always seem to want what we can't have?..
....
....

Since Eve's deception in the Garden of Eden, the list of things people think they "just gotta have" has greatly increased. Man's desire to possess anything and everything continues to exist in the world today.

PROJECT: What do you "lust" for?

Go to almost any store and you can probably find something that you would really like to possess. Many Americans have stuff in their homes that they have hardly used. The list of things that we want to accumulate is virtually endless. Can you add to this list of things people "lust" for?

> Cars
>
> Entertainment systems
>
> Cool clothes
>
> Video games
>
> Skateboard equipment
>
> Athletic gear
>
> Jewelry
>
> ....
>
> ....
>
> ....

Worldly Patterns of Possessions • King Solomon searched for meaning in many things. He sought pleasure; he also sought possessions. Here is the report from his search.

Ecclesiastes 2:1-3
I thought in my heart, "Come now, I will test you with pleasure to find out what is good." But that also proved to be meaningless. "Laughter," I said, "is foolish. And what does pleasure accomplish?" I tried cheering myself with wine, and embracing folly – my mind still guiding me with wisdom. I wanted to see what was worthwhile for men to do under heaven during the few days of their lives.

Solomon in his search for meaning looked to pleasure and found there was nothing in it. Next he turned to possessions to find satisfaction.

Ecclesiastes 2:4-11
I undertook great projects: I built houses for myself and planted vineyards. I made gardens and parks and planted all kinds of fruit

trees in them. I made reservoirs to water groves of flourishing trees. I bought male and female slaves and had other slaves who were born in my house. I also owned more herds and flocks than anyone in Jerusalem before me. I amassed silver and gold for myself, and the treasure of kings and provinces. I acquired men and women singers, and a harem as well – the delights of the heart of man. I became greater by far than anyone in Jerusalem before me. In all this my wisdom stayed with me. I denied myself nothing my eyes desired; I refused my heart no pleasure. My heart took delight in all my work, and this was the reward for all my labor. Yet when I surveyed all that my hands had done and what I had toiled to achieve, everything was meaningless, a chasing after the wind; nothing was gained under the sun.

Wow! Look at all that Solomon had; and he ended by saying it was meaningless and there was no profit in it! Add to the list below why Solomon probably realized possessions were meaningless.

Temporary value

You die and they are left behind

....

....

....

....

"He Who Dies With The Most Toys Wins!"

This popular bumper sticker accurately describes an attitude the world seems to display toward "stuff." The more you can get the better off you will be. This statement caused some wise person to write, "He who dies with the most toys still dies!"

Why do you think people try to "get" all the stuff they can in life?...
....
....

What are some ways people flaunt the stuff they have?...
....
....

God's Perspective on Possessions • An ambassador receives his money from the
kingdom he represents. While living abroad he may find his home currency has different value than that of the foreign land he is visiting. As Ambassadors of Christ, we should share God's values concerning wealth and riches.

God is Our Provider

All wealth belongs to God. The whole world is God's. He is the source of all wealth.

Psalm 50:9-12

I have no need of a bull from your stall or of goats from your pens, for every animal of the forest is mine, and the cattle on a thousand hills. I know every bird in the mountains, and the creatures of the fields are mine. If I were hungry I would not tell you, for the world is mine, and all that is in it.

It is important to know who owns all the wealth. If you needed something, would you go ask your little brother or sister? Probably not because they don't have the cash – but your parents do. So you would ask **them**.

All wealth belongs to God. He is free to give it, take it and do whatever He wants with it. He made it all and it belongs to Him. We just get to use it from time to time – based on how trustworthy we are with it! We are like a bank – a wealthy person may bring his resources and entrust them to us. We have the privilege of using and investing those resources, but the money doesn't belong to us, the bank; it belongs to the customer. The customer can take his money back whenever he wants.

Have you ever thought about this, that everything you have really belongs to God? How would you live life differently knowing this fact? How will that affect your desires and purchase of things?................
....
....

Possessions on Earth are Temporary, but True Riches Last into Eternity

Proverbs 23:5

Cast but a glance at riches, and they are gone, for they will surely sprout wings and fly off to the sky like an eagle.

If you have a job, you have probably observed that fact. Your money is often spent before you even get your paycheck! This proverb reminds us that money is so temporary that, as soon as we glance at it, it escapes us. God is trying to let us know that life is too short to spend so much time trying to accumulate money.

God offers an everlasting source of riches that will not vanish.

Matthew 6:19-21

Do not store up for yourselves treasures on earth, where moth and rust destroy, and where thieves break in and steal. But store up for yourselves treasures in heaven, where moth and rust do not destroy and where thieves do not break in and steal. For where your treasure is, there your heart will be also.

Two Types of Riches

Treasures on Earth

1. Enjoy it for 70 years or so while alive on earth.
2. Can be destroyed or ruined.
3. Can be stolen or taken away.
4. Jesus tells us not to pursue earthly treasure.

Treasures in Heaven

1. Have to wait 70 years or so to enjoy – but it lasts for eternity.
2. Cannot be destroyed or ruined.
3. Cannot be stolen or taken away.
4. Jesus tells us to pursue heavenly treasure.

1
2
3
4
5
6
a
b

PROJECT: Where is Your Heart?

Jesus said that where your treasure is, there your heart is also.

What are some behaviors and thoughts that describe a person whose heart and treasure is on the earth?

....

....

What do you think a person acts like when his heart and treasure are in heaven?

....

....

Because God's values are different from the world's, many things exist that God says are more valuable than money. Let's take a look at some of these.

Four Things Greater Than Money •

A Relationship with God

Proverbs 15:16
Better a little with the fear of the Lord than great wealth with turmoil.

It should be obvious to a Christian that a relationship with God is more important than money. If we had no relationship with Him, we would never have salvation and a life with Him in heaven for eternity. Why then do you suppose some Christian students decide their life's occupations based solely on how much money they can make, instead of how they can invest treasures in heaven?

....

....

....

....

Love

Proverbs 15:17
Better a meal of vegetables where there is love than a fattened calf with hatred.

In most cultures, meat is considered more valuable and desirable than vegetables (unless of course you are a vegetarian). The fattened calf was a sign of wealth and celebration. What is the point, however, if love is not present?

This is like a woman who marries a man because he is wealthy and can provide her with the best life offers – yet she has no love for him. Many great tragedies have been written about those who have forsaken love to get some material pleasure. A good plot for a love story is one that deals with a woman struggling between the man she loves (who is not able to provide for her), versus a man whom she does not love who has the ability to give her everything. Love is better than anything this world offers.

Wisdom

Proverbs 16:16
How much better to get wisdom than gold, to choose understanding rather than silver!

To see life God's way is more valuable than any amount of money. In the first book of Kings, God promised to give Solomon anything he asked for. Solomon chose wisdom, and as a reward received riches as well.

A Good Reputation

Proverbs 22:1
A good name is more desirable than great riches, to be esteemed is better than silver or gold.

Our society is full of people, both rich and poor, who have lost their reputations because of accusations (some true and others false). No amount of money can restore the public's perception of them. To lose the value of your good name is truly a great loss.

God's Counsel on Earning Money • There are only 3 ways to get more money.

Inherit It
This is an easy way to get money, but if there isn't anybody to give it, you are out of luck. An inheritance is nice, but you can't depend on that; you need to be able to control your money-making abilities.

Steal It

Obviously you can take money that doesn't belong to you, but what you are doing is wrong. Stolen wealth lacks value according to God's Word.

Proverbs 10:2
Ill-gotten treasures are of no value, but righteousness delivers from death.

Grow It (by Earning Wages)

Sounds hard and risky, but this is the last option we have. To a certain extent you can control how it grows and how you earn it. There are some principles to consider in earning a living.

Earn Money Legally and Gradually

Whether you work honestly or dishonestly, you still have to work. God tells us to work honestly. Drug dealers and thieves work hard for their cash – but it dwindles away. Honest money goes further.

Proverbs 13:11
Dishonest money dwindles away, but he who gathers money little by little makes it grow.

God also advises us to earn money little by little to make it grow. Many people believe in "get rich quick" schemes. Most people lose more than they make. Do not try to take the easy way out – you will lose over time.

Do you need some extra cash right now? What are some small things that you can do to gradually earn some money?...
....
....
....

Work Hard

Since you will have to work, you might as well give it everything you've got. Shoddy work and laziness will rob you over time. Hard work will give you opportunities to advance and bring a profit from your labor.

Proverbs 14:23
All hard work brings a profit, but mere talk leads only to poverty.

Save It

In our society we learn to "get it now." Credit cards and loans make us able to "purchase what we don't have to impress people we don't like." We use credit to buy things for which we don't have money at the present time. The problem is, living on credit devours future money. Many people get into a cycle they can't get out of. Save money for the hard times in life, and only buy what you can afford.

Proverbs 21:20
In the house of the wise are stores of choice food and oil, but a foolish man devours all he has.

If you have a job, are you saving any money? If not, could you save a small amount and put it in the bank? How much do you think you could save?..
....
....

A Tale of Two Twins: Making Your Money Work for You!

Because of the effect of compound interest, it makes more sense to save a small amount of money regularly for a long period of time than to save a much larger amount of money over a smaller period of time. To see an example of how this works, let's take two twin brothers, John and David. John decided that he wanted to start saving early, so he got a job when he turned 15 and was able to save $250 that first year. He plans to continue to faithfully add $250 a year to his account every year until he turns 65. Over the 50 year period, assuming that John can earn an average of 6% annually on his money, his $250 a year will grow to over $76,900. It's not a fortune; but it's not too shabby for $250 a year. As John gets older, the amount he is able to save will probably increase -- making his total savings even greater.

John's brother David, on the other hand, doesn't understand the importance of saving his money when he is young. He spends everything he earns on video games and compact discs. He figures that he will wait until he is older to start saving his money. When he turns 35, he looks at his empty bank account and decides it is time to start saving. Since he is older, David decides to put back $500 a year, twice as much as his brother is saving annually. When he turns 65, assuming the same 6% rate of interest, David will only have about $41,900 from his $500 dollar investments. To catch up with John, David would have had to save over $900 a year—almost four times as much as John saved. Which brother was wiser in managing his money?

John		David	
Saves $250/yr from age 15 to age 65		Saves $500/yr from age 35 to age 65	
Age 15	$250	Age 15	$0
20	1,494	20	0
25	3,493	25	0
30	6,168	30	0
35	9,748	35	500
40	14,539	40	2,988
45	20,950	45	6,986
50	29,530	50	12,336
55	41,012	55	19,496
60	56,377	60	29,078
65	76,939	65	41,901

PROJECT: Where is Your Money Going?

Assuming that you have money, where is it going? It is a good idea to periodically check how you are spending it so that you can decide if that is really how you want it used. Some people call that a budget. Take a few minutes to figure out where your income is going.

How much do you earn a month? $........................

How much do you spend a month?

On giving to God and others	$........................
On food	$........................
On movies, music, video games, etc.	$........................
On girlfriend/boyfriend	$........................
On	$........................
On	$........................
On	$........................
Total Expenses	$........................

Subtract Expenses from Income (Do you have anything left over?) $........................

Look at the budget you have just prepared. If you didn't have anything left over at the end of the month, you obviously need to make some changes. If you did have money remaining, did you save that money or did you spend it? Are you happy with the way you are spending your money? Do you need to make more money? Do you need to save more money? What adjustments (if any) do you want to make?..
....
....

43

Give It

It doesn't seem to make sense that giving money will help it increase. Yet, that is exactly what God says will happen! What's more, we will receive far more than money: true riches and blessings from God. Consider these two ways to give.

a.) Give to the Lord

Since everything is God's in the first place, why shouldn't we offer back to Him some of what He has given us? In this way we truly show God where our hearts are. Giving to the Lord also enables us to keep the church and its ministries going so that others can hear about how wonderful God is.

b.) Give to Others

Some people have been blessed with the ability to give large sums of money to those in need. Instead of hoarding what you have, give to others in need. God will bless you with true riches.

Proverbs 11:24
One man gives freely, yet gains even more; another withholds unduly, but comes to poverty.

b.) Give to the Lord

Since everything is God's in the first place, why shouldn't we offer back to Him some of what He has given us? In this way we truly show God where our hearts are. Giving to the Lord also enables us to keep the church and its ministries going so that others can hear about how wonderful God is.

Proverbs 3:9-10
Honor the Lord with your wealth, with the first fruits of all your crops; then your barns will be filled to overflowing, and your vats will brim over with new wine.

Are you giving any of your earnings to others or to the Lord?..
....
....

Why do you think that God promises to bless those who give generously?...............................
....
....

Conclusion • The world spends much of its time seeking material possessions and wealth, often at the expense of what God considers true riches.

Since God is the owner of all created things, we need to adopt His values and His perspective on wealth. God is more concerned with eternal things and less with temporary, material items. Our lives and the lives of others are riches that will last into eternity. Our use of material wealth should be to live modestly and advance the eternal agenda of God.

As Ambassadors of the Kingdom of Heaven, we should be more concerned with the treasures in our permanent home (heaven) and not of the world we serve.

notes:

45

to be, was a victim of one of my infamous "vapor gifts." My first idea for "vapor gifts" came when I was fourteen years old. Family finances weren't

chapter 5

YOU ARE NO
LONGER A
SLAVE *but*
AN HEIR

PATTERNS OF POSITION

Worldly Patterns of Position • The world's pattern of popularity, fame and success differ from God's perspective. Our society ranks people according to status based on many factors that go against God's values. Let's look once again at 1 John.

1 John 2:15-17
Do not love the world or anything in the world. If anyone loves the world, the love of the Father is not in him. For everything in the world – the cravings of sinful man, the lust of his eyes and the boasting of what he has and does – comes not from the Father but from the world. The world and its desires pass away, but the man who does the will of God lives forever.

What does "Boasting of What He Has and Does" Mean?

This worldly characteristic sums up the desire of man to be esteemed in the eyes of others. As humans we have a desire to advance our position in the eyes of others.

In the Garden of Eden, Eve saw the fruit from the forbidden tree as a means of elevating her present position in life.

Genesis 3:6
When the woman saw that the fruit of the tree was good for food and pleasing to the eye and also desirable for gaining wisdom, she took some and ate it....

Eve's desire to change her position in life ("you will be 'like God,'" Satan promised) only caused her to become ashamed and embarrassed. Her position in life as God's creation in His likeness was truly all she needed, but she was deceived. The world is deceived as to what success, status, and achievement really are.

Describe how the world might judge the social position of a person based upon the characteristics listed below.

Color of skin ....

Nationality ....

Academic background ....

Wealth ....

Location of home ....

Looks ....

Age...

Accomplishments ....

Talent ....

PROJECT: Moving Up in the World?

Our world tells us that we need to do certain things for our lives to matter. If we don't do these things, we don't enjoy the status that others enjoy. Write down your thoughts why students might think they could improve their status through the following:

Involve themselves in activities..

....

....

Choose high-paying occupations...

....

....

Do stupid things like drugs to prove they are cool..

....

....

Sleep around to get the right guy or girl..

....

....

What are the dangers of seeking status the world's way?..

....

....

God's Perspective on Position •
God has given us a great position in His kingdom! Let's take a moment to see the position that we have in Christ. Let's see the position that Christians have in God's eyes – the only eyes that matter!

God Views Christians as His Own Children!

1 John 3:1
How great is the love the Father has lavished on us, that we should be called children of God! And that is what we are! The reason the world does not know us is that it did not know him.

You may not have been born into the most prominent family on earth, but as a follower of Christ, you are considered one of His children. There is no better family to be a part of than to be a part of God's family tree.

God Views Us as His Friends!

John 15:13-15
Greater love has no one than this, that he lay down his life for his friends. You are my friends if you do what I command. I no longer call you servants, because a servant does not know his master's business. Instead, I have called you friends, for everything that I learned from my Father I have made known to you.

You may not have the greatest friends in a human sense, but God Himself calls you His friend. No need to try to earn His acceptance, He chose you and won't flake out.

God Views Us as Heirs to His Kingdom!

Galatians 4:7
So you are no longer a slave, but a son; and since you are a son, God has made you also an heir.

You may not have all the wealth necessary to gain a position in the eyes of man, but you are an heir to the great treasure in eternity. When others' wealth have passed away you will be enjoying the true riches of heaven!

If God has positioned us in high places, how should we position ourselves to others?.............................

....

....

The Example of Christ • When seeking how to live, we must first look to the life of Christ. As God's Son, being fully God and man, he did everything correctly using the same abilities that we as humans possess. Let's see how Jesus positioned Himself before others.

Jesus Lowered Himself and Became Nothing in the Eyes of Man

Philippians 2:5-7
Your attitude should be the same as that of Christ Jesus: Who being in very nature God, did not consider equality with God something to be grasped, but made himself nothing, taking the very nature of a servant, being made in human likeness.

It is hard to believe that Christ, who was present at creation and was God's own Son, did not come to earth as a prince, a king, or a celebrity. Jesus Christ was no superstar. Instead He stripped himself of greatness to serve mankind. The prophet Isaiah foretold that Christ would have no stature or physical prowess that would make Him appealing in the eyes of man. He was born into the home of a carpenter. Jesus was as average-looking as a guy could be.

Jesus Taught His Disciples How to Position Themselves Before Others

Jesus was perfect, but his disciples were not. Many occasions arose as the twelve spent time with Jesus that required Jesus to remind them of God's perspective on status.

Mark 9:33-37
They came to Capernaum. When he was in the house, he asked them, "What were you arguing about on the road?" But they kept quiet because on the way they had argued about who was the greatest. Sitting down, Jesus called the Twelve and said, "If anyone wants to be first, he must be the very last, and the servant of all." He took a little child and had him stand among them. Taking him in his arms, he said to them, "Whoever welcomes one of these little children in my name welcomes me; and whoever welcomes me does not welcome me but the one who sent me."

To Become First, We Must Be Last!

Jesus wanted his disciples to not argue over who was better, but to consider themselves last.

When you must form a line, do you allow others to go before you or do you rush to the front of the line?

....

When you eat dinner at your house do you try to see that your parents and siblings are served before you?

....
....
....

Do you look for opportunities to put others first?...

....
....

To Improve Our Position God's Way, We Must Become a Servant to All

No doubt the disciples were vying for position on the road to Capernaum. Jesus told them that instead of improving their status so that they may receive service, they should serve.

PROJECT: Being Served and Serving Others
How have the following people served you?

Your parents: ....

....
....

Your teachers: ....

....
....

Your brother/sister: ....

....
....

Your best friend: ....

....
....

Your youth pastor/worker: ....

....
....

How could you serve the following people in the next week?

Your parents: ....

....

Your teachers: ....

....

Your brother/sister: ....

....

Your best friend: ....

....

Your youth pastor/worker: ....

....

....

Jesus Wanted The Disciples to Follow His Example

The disciples were confused by their worldly concepts of position. The mother of James and John approached Jesus (with her sons) regarding their position in the kingdom of heaven.

Matthew 20:20-28

Then the mother of Zebedee's sons came to Jesus with her sons and, kneeling down, asked a favor of him. "What is it you want?" he asked. She said, "Grant that one of these two sons of mine may sit at your right and the other at your left in your kingdom." "You don't know what you are asking," Jesus said to them. "Can you drink the cup I am going to drink?" "We can," they answered. Jesus said to them, "You will indeed drink from my cup, but to sit at my right or left is not for me to grant. These places belong to those for whom they have been prepared by my Father." When the ten heard about this, they were indignant with the two brothers. Jesus called them together and said, "You know that the rulers of the Gentiles lord it over them, and their high officials exercise authority over them. Not so with you. Instead, whoever wants to become great among you must be your servant, and whoever wants to be first must be your slave just as the Son of Man did not come to be served, but to serve, and to give his life as a ransom for many."

God is the Ultimate Authority and the Giver of Status!

James and John were seeking status from a human being. The world looks for status from other people. Jesus made it clear that no man had the authority to give true position other than God Himself.

What are some ways people look to others to improve their status?...

....

....

Real Heavenly Position Comes by Dying to Yourself

The world considers those who sacrifice themselves for others to be weak. "Look out for number one," they will say. Jesus did not look out for himself, but for others. He allowed himself to be humiliated and killed in order to put others first. If we are going to truly seek heavenly status, then we must die to our desires and serve others.

Add to this list some things you or other people consider "beneath" you.

> Cleaning Toilets
>
> Giving money to beggars
>
> Spending time with lonely people
>
> Tying other people's shoes
>
> ....
>
> ....

Matthew 23:1-12

Then Jesus said to the crowds and to his disciples: "The teachers of the law and the Pharisees sit in Moses' seat. So you must obey them and do everything they tell you. But do not do what they do, for they do not practice what they preach. They tie up heavy loads and put them on men's shoulders, but they themselves are not willing to lift a finger to move them. "Everything they do is done for men to see: They make their phylacteries wide and the tassels on their garments long; they love the place of honor at banquets and the most important seats in the synagogues; they love to be greeted in the marketplaces and to have men call them 'Rabbi.' "But you are not to be called 'Rabbi,' for you have only one Master and you are all brothers. And do not call anyone on earth 'father,' for you have one Father, and he is in heaven. Nor are you to be called 'teacher,' for you have one Teacher, the Christ. The greatest among you will be your servant. For whoever exalts himself will be humbled, and whoever humbles himself will be exalted.

53

Learning From The Parable of the Good Samaritan •

Luke 10:25-37

On one occasion an expert in the law stood up to test Jesus. "Teacher," he asked, "what must I do to inherit eternal life?" "What is written in the Law?" he replied. "How do you read it?" He answered: "'Love the Lord your God with all your heart and with all your soul and with all your strength and with all your mind'; and, 'Love your neighbor as yourself.'" "You have answered correctly," Jesus replied. "Do this and you will live." But he wanted to justify himself, so he asked Jesus, "And who is my neighbor?" In reply Jesus said: "A man was going down from Jerusalem to Jericho, when he fell into the hands of robbers. They stripped him of his clothes, beat him and went away, leaving him half dead.

A priest happened to be going down the same road, and when he saw the man, he passed by on the other side. So too, a Levite, when he came to the place and saw him, passed by on the other side. But a Samaritan, as he traveled, came where the man was; and when he saw him, he took pity on him. He went to him and bandaged his wounds, pouring on oil and wine. Then he put the man on his own donkey, took him to an inn and took care of him. The next day he took out two silver coins and gave them to the innkeeper. 'Look after him,' he said, 'and when I return, I will reimburse you for any extra expense you may have.' "Which of these three do you think was a neighbor to the man who fell into the hands of robbers?" The expert in the law replied, "The one who had mercy on him." Jesus told him, "Go and do likewise."

This Pharisee was not truly seeking to speak to Jesus, but was seeking to justify his own behavior. This Pharisee most likely knew he couldn't meet every need in the world, but there were many needs around him that he was ignoring. "Surely I cannot be responsible for all these people," he most likely thought, so he sought to justify his inaction. Christ's response was most interesting, particularly because the first two characters in the parable that encounter the injured man were "religious" people. The Samaritan people were the victims of racial prejudice because they were the result of mixed marriages between Jews and Gentiles. The Samaritan would be the least likely person to be the hero of the story, yet he was the one who took action. What did the Samaritan man do that was right?

He *SAW* the Need
Yes, the first two passersby saw the man, but they did not see the need. Perhaps they thought "Someone else will come by and help this man." Maybe they were so consumed with their own plans they failed to notice that the man was desperately injured.

Are you looking for opportunities to serve others?...
....
....

What are some needs in your family, church, school, or community that you can meet?.....................
....
....

He *WENT* to the Need
The other two passersby took extra measures to avoid coming in contact with the man. Chances are the man was not in a convenient location to reach. Jesus said the Samaritan went to him. This meant that the Samaritan had to stop what he was doing and make time for the man. He had to change his plans.

The injured man did not approach the Samaritan; the Samaritan took the initiative to go to him.

Do you go out of your way to serve others in need?...

....

....

Where would you need to go to meet the needs you listed above?......................................

....

....

What might you need to give up?...

....

....

He *SERVED* to the Extent He Could

The Samaritan gave the man food, water and bandaged him. The man was in need of much more than the Samaritan could provide, but to the extent he was able, he took care of the needs. When the Samaritan realized he could not do more, he found him a place to stay and provided for his care.

There are many needs in the world, and it is clear that we cannot be a part of them all. But to the extent that we are able, we need to be involved. The typical reaction to the many needs around us is that we do nothing.

What are some things you can do to serve others according to your ability?.....................

....

....

That's Heavy, Man!

During the Hippie era of the 60's, the jargon used for something awesome was, "That's heavy, man." God instructs us to do something "real heavy" in the Ten Commandments. The fifth command gives us this instruction, but also promises something in return: • *Exodus 20:12 "Honor your father and your mother, so that you may live long in the land the LORD your God is giving you."*

The term he uses for "honor" comes from a Hebrew word meaning, "to be heavy," "to be weighty," "to be glorious," even, "to be rich." God wants students to hold their parents in high regard, to value them, to treasure them as something expensive. That is part of God's Pattern of Position: honor your parents.

Our parents aren't the only ones for us to honor. Whom else are we to show high respect for? The Bible tell us that...

We are to honor God with our wealth. (Proverbs 3:9)
We are to honor God with our bodies. (I Corinthians 6:20)

>

actually spend money on gifts? What if we just gave thoughts? Vapor gifts! We could give everybody what we want to give them regardless of

We are to honor our employers [masters]. (Malachi 1:6)
We are to honor our church leaders. (I Timothy 5:17)
We are to honor the King [here in our country -- the President]. (I Peter 2:17)

And, by the way, the Bible tells us to submit to everyone in governing authority over us. (Romans 13:1-6) This could not only include the government, but also the police, our teachers, etc. The passage goes on to summarize in verse 7, *"Give everyone what you owe him: If you owe taxes, pay taxes; if revenue, then revenue; if respect, then respect; if honor, then honor."* We are to give honor even though we might not like the person involved!

And finally, when it comes to honoring others, this next verse tells us where the real challenge lays honor every-one! • *Romans 12:10 Be devoted to one another in brotherly love. Honor one another above yourselves.*
Now, that's real heavy, man! But, there's always a promise to help us. Jesus says, "My Father will honor the one who serves me." (John 12:26) That's a goal worth working towards!

Conclusion • The world's perspective of status is based on the position achieved or given in the eyes of other people. According to God's Word, God alone is the giver of status. As Christians we all have a significant position in God's family.

While the world esteems those who become well-known for a variety of reasons, God tells us that to become first we must become last. As Ambassadors of the Kingdom of Heaven we must serve others and treat them the way we would want to be treated ourselves.

notes:

chapter 6

GO AND MAKE
DISCIPLES
OF ALL THE NATIONS

PATTERNS OF PURPOSE

Worldly Patterns of Purpose • Have you ever noticed that many people seem to be hopeless? They have gotten lost in the world's perspective of living. The world's pattern basically says, "There is no purpose for life." But we know better; we all know there has to be some meaning. The people of the world waste much of their time searching for this.

PROJECT: Meaning in Life

Describe why people might look for meaning in life in the following activities:

Political causes: ....

Animal rights: ....

Human rights: ....

Environmental issues: ....

Acts of kindness: ....

Donating money: ....

Giving their time to a worthy cause: ....

These activities, even though they may be good, do not satisfy the deep need we all have to find meaning in life. They eventually lead to frustration.

As people get frustrated in their pursuit to find a purpose for living they turn to many self-destructive behaviors to numb their pain.

Can you add to the list below of ways people attempt to escape their feelings of purposelessness?

Drugs

Addictions to video games and other activities

Weapons at school

Crimes against others

Suicide

....

....

....

God's Purpose and Plan for Mankind • The good news is that God has a plan for our lives – and it is a mighty good one.

Jeremiah 29:11
For I know the plans I have for you," declares the LORD, "plans to prosper you and not to harm you, plans to give you hope and a future.

God's plan for us is that we trust Him for our future. When we place our trust in Christ to save us of our sin, He calls us friends, and we become His children. He tells us that He is preparing a place for us beyond this life, and can give us abundant life at this time too. Sounds like a great plan to me!

The First Mission

Genesis 1:28
God blessed them and said to them, "Be fruitful and increase in number; fill the earth and subdue it. Rule over the fish of the sea and the birds of the air and over every living creature that moves on the ground."

When God created man and woman He gave them specific commands to fulfill.

Increase in Number
God's plan was bigger than Adam and Eve having many children. Because there was no sin in the world at that time, each child born would be born into a relationship with God. This was not just a command to multiply, but to increase those who followed God.

a.) How Sin Messed This Up

After sin entered the world, mankind was no longer born into a perfect relationship with God. Sin meant death and separation. This created the need for a Savior, and ambassadors who would tell others how to enter into a right relationship.

Master the Earth

Adam and Eve were told to subdue the earth. God desired that they be creative and learn all they could about His creation. They were also instructed to rule over every living thing.

a.) How Sin Messed This Up

Once sin entered the world, Adam and Eve no longer were given the privilege of having dominion. They were ejected from the Garden never to return. Animals would now fear them. Work would become toilsome, and roses would have thorns. Childbirth would be painful. Because Christ died for our sins, we have a chance to live forever. Christ will return someday, and bring in a new heaven and new earth, and will rule over the earth at His second coming.

The Present Task

Jesus has come and offered His life up for the world. It is a free gift and He has commanded us to tell the world!

The Great Commission

Matthew 28:16 -20

Then the eleven disciples went to Galilee, to the mountain where Jesus had told them to go. When they saw him, they worshiped him; but some doubted. Then Jesus came to them and said, "All authority in heaven and on earth has been given to me. Therefore go and make disciples of all nations, baptizing them in the name of the Father and of the Son and of the Holy Spirit, and teaching them to obey everything I have commanded you. And surely I am with you always, to the very end of the age."

Before Christ ascended to heaven He instructed the disciples to go and make more disciples. Christ has been given all authority to do this. Now, realize that nobody takes commands from "just anyone." We only do what those in a position of authority tell us to do. Christ has been given authority on heaven and earth making Him the one to watch! We no longer need to worry about others telling us what to do, Christ is the one in charge! Notice the specifics of these commands.

a.) GO!

Are we told to wait for people to come to us or call us on the phone asking how they can become a disciple? NO! We are told to go, and that means we take the initiative. We have been given a mission; we don't just "hope" it happens, we are constantly taking action to see that it occurs. Christ assumes that we will go. His words literally are, "As you are going, make disciples..."

Why don't people take action when it comes to this clear command of Christ?.................................
....
....

b.) Make Disciples

Our goal is not to just get somebody to pray a prayer or become "saved." The objective we have been given is to "make disciples." That means to share Christ in such a way that people can follow Him. We need to work with people over time to show them how to live for Christ and to follow Him.

What is the difference between winning a convert and making a disciple?.................................
....
....

Winning Converts vs. Making Disciples

If you could preach to 100,000 people a day and have 4% of your audience make a decision for Christ, it would take 4,108 years to reach the world for Christ. If we really want to reach the world for Christ, we need to use the methodology of Christ. Jesus invested His life in a small group of twelve men who, in turn, invested their lives in discipling others. If you could disciple one new believer for one year, and then the two of you disciple two more new believers for a year, and then the four of you disciple four new believers for a year, and so on, the entire world could be reached with the gospel in 33 years!

c.) Baptize Them

Baptism is a symbol of our decision to follow Christ. There is nothing magical about baptism, but it is an act of obedience and testimony. Christ was baptized as an example for us to follow. Christ died, and was buried, and rose again to a new life. In baptism we identify with Christ's death and resurrection. We are showing the world that we have died to the old life, and are now living for Him.

d.) Teach Them

More than just a one-time knock on a door, we need to continually help others grow in their understanding of God. This is one reason we attend church. We need to learn from other Christians and to hear God's Word practically applied to our lives.

Christ is with You

Jesus said that He would be with you as you carry out this mission. Isn't that exciting news! We do not need to be afraid or worry that we will fail, because Christ promises to be with us.

"Preach Christ at all times - if necessary use words!" – Francis of Assisi

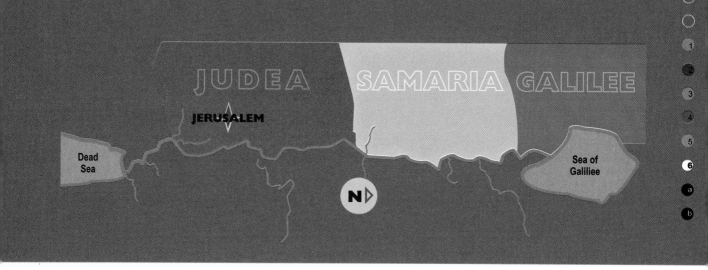

A Model for Outreach •

Acts 1:8-9
But you will receive power when the Holy Spirit comes on you; and you will be my witnesses in Jerusalem, and in all Judea and Samaria, and to the ends of the earth. After he said this, he was taken up before their very eyes, and a cloud hid him from their sight.

When Jesus spoke to them, the disciples were at that time in Jerusalem. But they then spread out to the outlying areas of Judea and Samaria. Ultimately, the disciples traveled across the world to share the good news of Jesus Christ.

The model given here encourages us to start where we presently are in life. We can share the news with those close to us. As time goes on, we will have influence and opportunity in other parts of life and eventually locations all around the world.

At Home (Jerusalem)
Jesus told his disciples to start in Jerusalem. Think about what had just occurred in Jerusalem. Jesus (their leader) had been executed by people who thought that he and his followers were trying to start a rebellion. It would have been much easier for the disciples if Jesus had told them to start in Africa! The disciples would be persecuted and misunderstood as long as they stayed in Jerusalem. If you go back home and start to live a changed life and have an influence for Christ, you will be persecuted and misunderstood too.

How can you be Christ's ambassador in your home?..
....
....
....

63

At School (Judea)

Judea was the region where Jerusalem was located. The Judeans had a similar religious and cultural background to the disciples. Jesus asked the disciples to take his message to people who were familiar to them. In your school, you have the opportunity to share the good news about Jesus with other students who face the same challenges and problems that you do.

How can you be Christ's ambassador in your school?...
....
....

In My Community (Samaria)

Samaria was a region that was just north of Judea. Unlike Judea, however, the Samaritans were not like the disciples at all. They had a completely different cultural and religious heritage. In fact, the Judeans hated the Samaritans. (Do you remember the story of the good Samaritan from the last chapter?) As you take the message and life of Christ out into your community, you will have to face people who are different from you, people who misunderstand you, maybe even people who hate you.

How can you be Christ's ambassador in your community?...
....
....

How can you be Christ's ambassador to those who are not like you?...
....
....

In the World (Ends of the Earth)

Jesus has called us to take His message to the whole world. That doesn't mean that every Christian is supposed to go overseas. There are people right next door to you or down the street who probably don't know Jesus. While you may be focusing your attention on the person next door, don't forget about the people across the globe. Maybe God is asking you to go on a mission trip with your youth group. Or maybe He is asking you to support a missionary overseas with your prayers or your gifts. The point is, we all should be involved in taking the message of Christ to the ends of the earth.

How can you be Christ's ambassador to the world?..
....
....

Conclusion • God has a plan for each of us. Using our special talents and abilities, God desires us to share with others that Jesus died for their sin and offers a better way to live. As ambassadors we cannot take our mission lightly. In all we do we must actively be making disciples.

notes:

APPENDIX Worship

The following appendix is intended to give an overview of different aspects of worship.

Introduction • Throughout the last chapters we have looked at how God's wisdom and mission for us is different from that of the worldly system that sets itself up against God. We are different when it comes to pleasure, possessions, position, and purpose. We are also different from the world in our worship. As humans we were designed to worship. The object worshiped may be different but all mankind will worship something!

In its simplest definition worship means to give worth to something or someone. People attribute worth to all sorts of things, yet the only thing that truly is worth anything is God. As Christians, our highest worth is in God, but people living according to the world place worth on other people and things.

What are some things people worship (or "worthship") other than God?.....................................
....
....

As Christians We Are Commanded To Worship God Only! •

Exodus 20:3-6

You shall have no other gods before me. You shall not make for yourself an idol in the form of anything in heaven above or on the earth beneath or in the waters below. You shall not bow down to them or worship them; for I, the LORD your God, am a jealous God, punishing the children for the sin of the fathers to the third and fourth generation of those who hate me, but showing love to a thousand generations of those who love me and keep my commandments.

In our society people use the word "god" to mean many different things. It may refer to a "higher power" or a "supreme" force out there. Our eternal God is very concerned that we do not worship anyone or anything other than Him. God did not allow images of stone or any material to be made of Him for fear people would worship the object! God has a personality and He desires worshipers who know Him for who He is and what He has done.

What Does It Take To Worship God? • The worship of God in the Old Testament revolved around sacrifices of animals brought to the priest at the tabernacle. The animals were slain and offered to God, either as an offering for sin, or perhaps as an offering of thanks. The best example from the New Testament of what worship is relates to Paul's challenge from the book of Romans.

Romans 12:1
Therefore, I urge you, brothers, in view of God's mercy, to offer your bodies as living sacrifices, holy and pleasing to God--this is your spiritual act of worship.

From his challenge we can learn some Principles of Worship.

Principles of Worship •

l. Worship is a Response to God's Character and What He has Done
Therefore, I urge you, brothers, *in view of God's mercy...*

Worship is what we do because of an encounter with God. Because God is merciful and has shown us mercy, we worship Him. Paul could have easily placed any of God's amazing and unique characteristics in place of mercy and the statement would be true.

2. Worship is an Intentional Act of the Will
Therefore, *I urge you*, brothers, in view of God's mercy, *to offer...*

Nobody just happens to worship God or His son Jesus. People worship as an act of their will. Worship must be done intentionally and not casually.

3. Worship Involves Surrender and Sacrifice
Therefore, I urge you, brothers, in view of God's mercy, to offer *your bodies as living sacrifices, holy and pleasing...*

In the Old Testament worshipers of God were required to make blood sacrifices of animals. There was a price to be paid in both money to purchase the animal or raise it and a cost in the loss of life. God asks us to offer ourselves as living sacrifices, that means that we offer our lives and our desires to Him.

The sacrificial animal was required to measure up to certain standards. We too should offer ourselves as holy and pleasing sacrifices.

4. Worship Requires Interaction with God

Therefore, I urge you, brothers, in view of God's mercy, to offer your bodies as living sacrifices, holy and pleasing *to God...*

Worship is interactive. Worship is not a presentation for God but is something that is done in His presence. If God is not there to accept your offering then it is meaningless. Worship is an intimate encounter with God.

God Is Seeking Worshipers! •

John 4:23-24
Yet a time is coming and has now come when the true worshipers will worship the Father in spirit and truth, for they are the kind of worshipers the Father seeks. God is spirit, and his worshipers must worship in spirit and in truth.

It is interesting to note that God is not seeking worship – He is seeking worshipers. God desires us! Jesus shares with us two aspects of the worshiper He is seeking. He wants worshipers who can worship in spirit and in truth.

In Spirit

We have never seen God or Jesus face to face, yet we are connected to Him through our spirit. The spirit is a mysterious part of who we are that is difficult to understand at times. It is our spirit that makes us different than the animals or any other living organism.

God has also given us the gift of His Holy Spirit. When you recognize your sinfulness and need for God to pay for that sin through the death of His Son, you are united with Christ in spirit. It is possible to worship God without being united with Him in spirit. It is important that we worship in spirit.

In Truth

God does not want us to disengage our mind nor to worship Him in falsehood or deception. God's Word is our source of truth here on earth. It is important to understand that we grow in our ability and understanding of worship as we learn more about His Word. It is difficult to worship God if you are not staying in touch with the truth found in His Word.

Pursuing God •

James 4:8a
Come near to God and he will come near to you.

Many people are waiting for God to find them, yet James challenges us to pursue God. Since worship is the result of an encounter with God, if we are not seeking Him and His presence, worship will be difficult to accomplish. The first step in our worship is to come near to Him.

How shall we pursue Him?

#1 Confessing of our Sins •

James 4:8b
Wash your hands, you sinners, and purify your hearts, you double-minded.

James immediately follows his challenge to pursue God with a challenge to confess sin. Sin separates us from being able to worship.

Psalm 5: 4-5
You are not a God who takes pleasure in evil; with you the wicked cannot dwell. The arrogant cannot stand in your presence; you hate all who do wrong.

Psalm 51:14-15
Save me from my bloodguilt , O God, the God who saves me, and my tongue will sing of your righteousness. O Lord, open my lips, and my mouth will declare your praise.

It makes sense, then, that if we want to draw near to God in worship we must confess our sin before Him and seek forgiveness. God promises us that if we confess our sins He will forgive us.

What are some wrong thoughts or actions you need to confess before God?.................................
....
....

#2 Adoring God's Person and Accomplishments • Let's take a look at
who God is and how we have experienced Him in our lives.

Knowing God

PROJECT: What are some names or character traits of God?
God has been given many names that reflect His character. Your father calls you his child; to your teacher you may be a student; to a politician you may be a citizen. But no matter what "title" you have,

you are the same person. Look through the list of some of the names or titles we have for God. Circle the names that are most meaningful to you at this time.

Hebrew Names of God and their Meaning:

Elohim - Plurality in Unity

El - The Strong One

Elah - An Oak

Eloah - The Adorable One

El Elyon - God Most High

El Roi - The Lord That Seeth

El-Elohe-Israel - God of Israel

El Olam - God of Eternity

El Shaddai - The Almighty, All Sufficient God

Adon-Adonai - Jehovah Our Ruler

Jah - The Independent One

Jehovah - The Eternal, Ever-loving One

Jehovah-Elohim - The Majestic Omnipotent God

Jehovah-Hoseenu - The Lord Our Maker

Jehovah-Jireh - The Lord Will Provide

Jehovah-Rophi - The Lord, The Physician

Jevovah-Nissi - The Lord our Banner

Jehovah M'Keddesh - The Lord Sanctifies

Jehovah-Eloheenu - Lord our God

Jehovah-Eloheka - Lord Thy God

Jehovah-Elohay - The Lord My God

Jehovah-Shalom - The Lord Our Peace

Jehovah-Tseboath - The Lord of Hosts

Jehovah-Rohi - The Lord My Shepherd

Jehovah-Tsidkenu - The Lord Our Righteousness

Jehovah-Makkeh - The Lord Shall Smite Thee

Jehovah-Gmolah - The God of Recompenses

Jehovah-Shammah - The Lord is There

Other Names Used of the Trinity:

> Father
> Lord
> Savior
> Comforter
> The One Who Comes Alongside To Help
> Alpha and Omega
> Advocate
> Friend
> Great Physician
> Prince of Peace
> Provider
> Lifter of My Soul
> Mighty Counselor
> Son of God
> Jesus
> The Christ
> I AM
> Helper
> My Light
> The Word
> The Way
> The Truth
> The Life
> The Lamb
> Teacher
> Peacemaker
> Creator

What are your favorite names for God?...
....
....

Character traits have been used to describe who God is and what He does for us. Circle the traits that are most meaningful to you at this time.

Character Traits:

Sovereign

All Knowing

All Powerful

All Present

Creative

Loving

Just

Faithful

Kind

Patient

Strong/Mighty

Righteous

Redeemer

Strong Tower

Refuge

Deliverer

Friend

True

Compassionate

Holy

Defender

Eternal

Exalted

Fortress

Forgiving

Wise

Take some time right now to thank God for some of the characteristics about Him that you really appreciate.

73

What are some ways you have seen God's character revealed in your life?......................................

....

....

Two Ways To Express Who God Is In Worship

Acknowledge God's blessings and character to others

Tell others about what God has done. Sing songs that speak of God's goodness in your life.

Acknowledge God's blessings and character to Him in adoration

Tell God how much you love who He is and what He has done. Sing songs about God to God directly, alone or with others.

#3 Giving Thanks • Another way we draw close to God in worship is by thanking Him for what He has done in our lives.

Thanksgiving honors God

Psalm 50:23
He who sacrifices thank offerings honors me, and he prepares the way so that I may show him the salvation of God.

Psalm 69: 30
I will praise God's name in song and glorify Him with thanksgiving.

We should thank God for everything.

Ephesians 5:20
...always giving thanks to God the Father for everything, in the name of Lord Jesus Christ.

What are some things we should be thankful for?

> **Answered prayer (2 Corinthians 1:10-11)**
>
> **Food (John 6:11)**
>
> **Salvation (I Corinthians 15:54-57)**

What are some things you are thankful for?...

....

....

#4 Being Obedient •

We show our love and devotion by obeying God's Word

John 14:23
Jesus replied, "If anyone loves me, he will obey my teaching. My father will love him, and he will come to him and make our home with him."

Ecclesiastes 12:13
Now all has been heard; here is the conclusion of the matter: Fear God and keep his commandments, for this is the whole duty of man.

Worship should be followed by a new desire to serve and obey God. As we worship we must realize that we are not performing for God, but we are in two-way communication with Him. As we confess our sin, and acknowledge the character of God, we might come to a new realization of actions we must take in our lives. We should not leave the experience of worship without some change occurring in our life.

What are some areas in your life in which God, in your time of worship, is calling you to be obedient?
....
....

#5 Waiting for God • In our microwave-fast-food society we are used to having everything

now. With overnight shipping, fax machines and the Internet, we rarely have to wait for anything. Even so, Scripture urges us to wait for God and His timing.

Psalm 27:14
Wait for the Lord; be strong and take heart and wait for the Lord.

Psalm 40:1
I waited patiently for the Lord; he turned to me and heard my cry.

As you pursue God, realize that you may have to wait for Him to show you what you need. Be strong knowing that God will hear your cry.

Can you remember a time when you had to wait on the Lord?..
....
....

#6 *Delighting in God* • There are two ways we can worship and pursue God. One is out of duty; the other is out of delight. Which one sounds more motivating?

God wants us to enjoy Him!

Psalm 37:4
Delight yourself in the Lord and he will give you the desires of your heart.

The second part of that verse sounds great! But what we often miss is that we are to delight in God. We can delight in Him by learning to find joy in serving and obeying Him! Worshiping God should not be chore!

Gather together in a group and celebrate God's goodness in your life. Worship can be a celebration of Who God is and What He has done in our lives!

Psalm 105:2
Sing to him, sing praise to him; tell of all his wonderful acts.

Psalm 95:1,2
Come, let us sing for joy to the Lord; let us shout aloud to the Rock of our salvation. Let us come before him with thanksgiving and extol him with music and song.

What are some things you remember God doing in your life that you can celebrate?...........................
....
....

Exploring Posture in Worship • Body Language is an important part of the communication process. Non-verbal communication is often more powerful and distinct than the spoken word!

For Instance:
- **You would have a hard time believing a person if they couldn't look you in the eye.**
- **You would feel uncomfortable if you made a move to shake someone's hand and they did not extend their hand to you.**
- **A person's expression will tell you more about their day than asking them.**
- **We've all hugged someone who doesn't want to be touched -- you can feel their lack**

rabbit which Jonathan had fed before we left. I was very upset at my parents. My brothers were mad too. Josh and Jeremy had homework to do;

of warmth.

Body language used to convey important attitudes:

- **Kneeling in the presence of a king shows respect for his powerful position.**
- **In war, raising hands high is a posture of surrendering your cause in exchange for your life.**
- **In courtship, getting on one knee to ask for a woman's hand in marriage is a demonstration of honor and submission.**

If non-verbal communication is so powerful, why do we fail to express these forms in our worship of God? Our posture in worship communicates the true expression of our inner self. Scripture gives us examples of appropriate posture/body language in worship.

Kneeling, Bowing Down, Raising Hands

Psalm 95:6
Come, let us bow down in worship, let us kneel before the LORD our Maker;

1 Kings. 8:22
Then Solomon stood before the altar of the LORD in front of the whole assembly of Israel, spread out his hands toward heaven,...

Psalm 134:2
Lift up your hands in the sanctuary and praise the LORD.

77

Romans 14:11
It is written: "As surely as I live," says the Lord, "every knee will bow before me; every tongue will confess to God."

The following is a list of non-verbal actions that have an outward effect on worship. How does your body language communicate the intention of your heart, and what are we saying to God during worship when we:

Kneel or bow..

Lift our head up..

Cross our arms across our chest...

Put our hands in our pockets..

Talk to a neighbor...

Pass notes...

Lay prostrate on the ground...

Look around..

Put on make-up...

Dance..

Raise our hands high...

It is important that we communicate with our whole self. When we worship, we should not be afraid to be so passionate for God that we limit ourselves to verbal expressions only. God is the Creator, the Eternal King, our Father. Let us honor and worship Him with all we have!

notes:

79

APPENDIX   *one month devotional*
by Christopher Lyon

WEEK 1

READ: *Romans 1* [monday-tuesday]

STUDY: "For although they knew God, they neither glorified him as God nor gave thanks to him, but their thinking became futile and their foolish hearts were darkened," (v. 21).

Reading the second half of Romans one is like reading a summary of our culture over the last 40 years. And since Paul wrote this almost 200 decades ago, apparently our society isn't the first to experience the pattern. Notice how it works.

1. Even though it's obvious from nature and their own hearts that God exists (v. 20), people find a way to convince themselves that He just ain't there (e.g. evolution) (v. 25).
2. People begin to worship created things (nature, themselves) instead of the Creator (v. 25).
3. God lets them wallow in their sin, and the society disintegrates into a mass of unthinking, unpleasant, and unrighteous people (v. 30-32) .The pattern keeps repeating itself. You've got to decide if you are going to live the pattern, hide from it, or fight it with love and the Truth.

PRAYER: Ask God for the courage to fight the pattern in your corner of society.

GOING DEEPER: Read Proverbs 17 and note verse 15 in light of recent court cases.

....

READ: *Romans 2,3* [wednesday-thursday]

STUDY: "This righteousness from God comes through faith in Jesus Christ to all who believe... For we maintain that a man is justified by faith apart from observing the law," (3:22,28).

Imagine if, in order to graduate from high school, you had to make it from kindergarten through your senior year without ever getting anything wrong. No missed questions on assignments or tests. Nothing less than an A+ on papers. No sick days. No tardies. No late assignments.

How many people would graduate? Maybe you know some people you think might come close, but no one can be perfect for 13 years of school. No one would ever graduate.

Same thing with God's Old Testament law for the Jews. It was God's standard for the righteous life. If you keep all those rules, your whole life, you could walk right into heaven.

In the end Paul says, "God gave us the law to show us just how useless it is for us to try and earn eternal life. We all deserve death.

The only righteous ones are those who've accepted it as a gift.

PRAYER: Thank God for giving you Jesus' perfect righteousness in place of your worthlessness.

GOING DEEPER: Ask God for wisdom, then read Proverbs 18.

READ: *Romans 4* [friday-sunday]

STUDY: "The man who does not work but trusts God who justifies the wicked, his faith is credited as righteousness," (v. 5).

Two men were sentenced to life with 100-pound iron balls chained to their ankles as punishment for a murdering, stealing crime spree.

One man dragged his weight from town to town, doing good wherever and whenever he could, hoping that one day the governor would see that the man had truly changed and release him.

The other dragged his weight to the governor's son, who took the key from his father's desk, released the man from the weight, and fastened the ball to his own ankle.

Three days later, the governor released his innocent son from the weight and invited the second man to his home as an honored guest.

To this day, the first man drags that weight around, refusing the invitation of the governor's son to take it away, and believing that his good works will one day earn his freedom.

Who are you trusting with your burden?

PRAYER: If you haven't, take your sin to Jesus, thank Him for paying the price for it, and accept His Father's invitation into the family.

GOING DEEPER: Write down three meaningful proverbs from Proverbs 19 and 20.

....

....

....

READ: *Romans 5* [monday-tuesday]

STUDY: "And we rejoice in the hope of the glory of God. Not only so, but we also rejoice in our sufferings, because we know that suffering produces perseverance; perseverance, character; and character, hope. And hope does not disappoint," (v. 2-5).

I think a lot of us miss the real key to living the Christian life on an everyday basis. We tend to think it's all in how much effort we put into it – Read! Study! Memorize! Do good! – or how many bad things we don't do.

But Paul seems to be saying the ultimate goal for a Christian is to get our hope in the right place. When we're young, we tend to put our hope in getting new stuff or human relationships or sex or accomplishments – not all bad things. They just can't satisfy us.

That's why today's verses say to rejoice in our sufferings and hard times. Because those times are the only thing that's gonna push us back to God and force us to place all our hope in Him. Then all that other stuff (reading, studying, memorizing) will come naturally. We'll want to get to know the One we're hoping in.

PRAYER: Ask God to help you hope in Him. But be ready to suffer.

GOING DEEPER: Read Proverbs 21 and be encouraged by verse 30.

READ: *Romans 6,7* [wednesday-thursday]

STUDY: "What shall we say then? Shall we go on sinning so that grace may increase? By no means! We died to sin; how can we live in it any longer?" (6:1,2).

I think I had to memorize this chapter for Bible class or at church camp when I was in sixth or seventh grade, and it did more for my thought life in junior and senior high than any other passage.

Like every teenage boy I've ever known, I struggled with controlling my thoughts, tempted to dwell on impure fantasies or images I'd seen on TV. A youth worker suggested I take this passage I had memorized and quote it in my head every time I started thinking about sensual stuff.

Guess what? It worked. Sometimes, I had to repeat the chapter to myself every five minutes, but it worked. The Holy Spirit was able to use the Word to purify my thoughts (Ps. 119:9).

So, no great insights today – just one practical suggestion. What have you got to lose?

PRAYER: Ask God to use the Bible to clean up your mind.

GOING DEEPER: Read Proverbs 22. If you re thinking about borrowing money, read verse 7 twice.

....

READ: *Romans 8* [friday-sunday]

STUDY: "In the same way, the Spirit helps us in our weakness. We do not know what we ought to pray for, but the Spirit himself intercedes for us with groans that words cannot express," (v. 26).

If you've ever read Douglas Adams' funny sci-fi book, Hitchhiker's Guide to the Galaxy, you've met the babble fish. In Adams' world, this intelligent little fish fits inside your ear and interprets whatever language someone is speaking into words you can understand.

The Holy Spirit takes this one step further, looking past our words (since we're really not very good at talking to God), and telling Him what we should be saying, what our hearts are crying out for.

That is so comforting to me. I don't have to be the most eloquent or well-spoken person to have an intimate and meaningful conversation with God. The Spirit takes care of that.

But I do have to open up my mouth and talk. If I don't pray something, the Spirit has nothing to pass on to Him. So the moral comes down to a Nike slogan. Just do it. Just talk to Him. And let the Spirit do His job.

PRAYER: Talk to God about whatever's on your mind.

GOING DEEPER: As part of your life-long wisdom quest, read Proverbs 23 and 24.

....

WEEK 3
READ: *Romans 9,10* [monday-tuesday]

STUDY: "That if you confess with you mouth, 'Jesus is Lord,' and believe in your heart that God raised him from the dead, you will be saved." (10:9).

Some people have read verses like this one and said to me, "How can it be that easy? Shouldn't someone have to change to become a Christian? Shouldn't you have to give up smoking and drinking? Shouldn't you have to read your Bible every night? Don't you have to prove it?"

And it is hard to accept – God offers me His love forever and all I have to do is confess my worthlessness and believe in His Son. For the people Paul was writing to, it was really hard to accept.

The Jews had been striving for a salvation based on works for hundreds of years, and now, all of a sudden, any non-Jew could be saved by simply accepting the gift.

Paul's point is, you could try to "prove your faithfulness" for a million years and you'd never be good enough.

PRAYER: Thank God for His gift to you.

GOING DEEPER: Read Proverbs 25 and memorize a verse that convicts you.

....

READ: Romans 11 [wednesday-thursday]

STUDY: "Who has ever given to God, that I God should repay him? For from him and through him and to him are all things. To him be the glory forever! Amen." (v. 35,36).

I remember watching a little kid, maybe four years old, "help" his dad work on the car. The little boy would get a serious look on his face, pick up tools and hand them to his dad (whether dad needed them or not), and then bang on the car with a hammer.

Was the little boy really helping? No. In fact, for the dad to get any work done at all, he had to either work quickly when the boy was distracted or hold the kid up in the engine, put a wrench in his hand, and turn the bolt with his hand over his son's.

So why did the dad put up with it? He could have done the job faster and better without the kid. But building that relationship, teaching his child, was more important to him than the job itself.

Your Father (God) works the same way. Can you really help Him do anything? Of course not. But He wants to work through you, to use you for His glory, to show you how He works. Let Him.

PRAYER: Ask God to work through you to do His will.

GOING DEEPER: Write down ten characteristics of a fool from Proverbs 26.

....

....

STUDY: "Be joyful in hope, patient in affliction, faithful in prayer." (v. 12).

This has become one of my favorite verses over the last few years. For me, it's kind of a three-legged stool for my attitude. If any of the legs fall out, my 'tude tumbles to the floor.

Leg one. Be joyful in hope. Some people stop quoting this phrase after the first two words. "Be joyful," they say. "You're a Christian." Yes, I am, but I can't just turn my joy on and off like a flashlight. The command here is, "Choose to be joyful about the fact that this life is short and you'll be with the One who loves you very soon." I can do that.

Leg two. Be patient in affliction. Notice that the verse just assumes you're going to have affliction. Don't freak when it happens it says. Wait for God to do His thing.

Leg three. Be faithful in prayer. I don't know why talking to my God faithfully is so hard for me. But I know that it's much tougher for me to be patient and joyful when I let that relationship slide. I gotta keep talking.

PRAYER: Ask God to give you three strong legs today.

GOING DEEPER: Read Proverbs 27 and 28. Don't miss 27:14, the official verse of Saturday morning.

WEEK 4
READ: *Romans 13,14* [monday-tuesday]

STUDY: "He who rebels against the authority is rebelling against what God has instituted, and those who do so will bring judgment on themselves," (13:2).

Generally speaking, our generation doesn't do very well with authority. Whether it's parents or cops or school teachers or church leaders, we tend to see them as an obstacle to getting what we want.

At best, we don't respect them. At worst, we see authority as the enemy.

That makes this passage pretty convicting. Paul just told us that all authority is put there by God. From the President to your math teacher, every last one of them was set up by Him. And whether they know it or not, they're serving His plan.

So, if we rebel against them – -unless they tell us to do something He told us not to – we're rebelling against God, too. Not a good idea.

Our task, then, is to let God direct our life through the authorities He's put there. Of course it's hard, but the younger we learn it, the better life will work in the long run.

PRAYER: Thank God for the authorities He's put in your life, naming them by name.

GOING DEEPER: Read Proverbs 29 and write out three good verses.

....

....

....

READ: *Romans 15* [wednesday-thursday]

STUDY: "Accept one another, then, just as Christ accepted you, in order to bring praise to God,"(v. 7).

This verse reads deceptively simple. Read it again. It's one of the toughest challenges in the Bible.

How did Christ accept you? In chapter five we read that "While we were still sinners, Christ died for us," (v. 8). Christ accepted us first. Before we accepted Him, before we were worthy, before we stopped doing it our way, He accepted us. No strings attached.

Now for the nasty questions: How do we accept each other? How do we accept that one kid in the group who talks too much and kind of smells sometimes? How do we accept that good-looking person with all the money and friends and clothes? How do we accept our parents?

Are you waiting for people to be good enough before you accept them? Are you waiting for them to accept you first? Are you waiting for the rest of the group to accept them?

Paul said "accept each other" like Jesus accepted you – first and with no strings. I guess we'd better change our thinking.

PRAYER: Ask God to give you the courage to love like Jesus.

GOING DEEPER: Read Proverbs 30 and count the things that are never satisfied.

READ: *Romans 16* [friday-sunday]

Man, we got this backwards, don't we? In the 90s, we're all pretty wise about evil and "innocent" (or unaware) about good. We might not actually participate in all the evil, but we sure know about it.

From TV and movies, I've learned how to murder people in hundreds of unique ways. From Oprah, Ricki, Maury, and Jerry, I've learned about every possible sexual perversion – and I've met the people who tried it. And that's only a little of the evil I know about.

But about being good – I haven't learned anything except from the Bible and the people who live it.

Maybe it's time for me to turn on less of the stuff that shows me all the interesting bad things out there and start tuning in to the one place that actually teaches me how to live right.

Or maybe not. What do you think?

PRAYER: Ask God to give you a passionate hunger for the good.

GOING DEEPER: Read Proverbs 31, and ask God to make you like that (if a girl) or give you one of those (if a guy).

notes:

89

ing His commands. Obedience is the key to opening up your relationship with Him.

The End

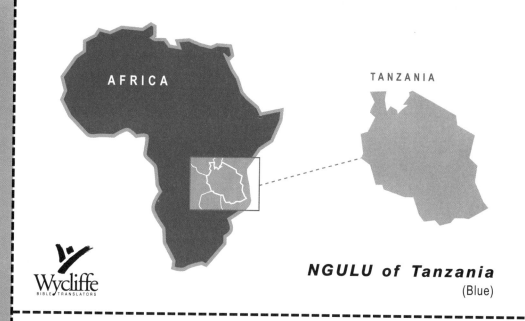

NGULU of Tanzania
(Blue)

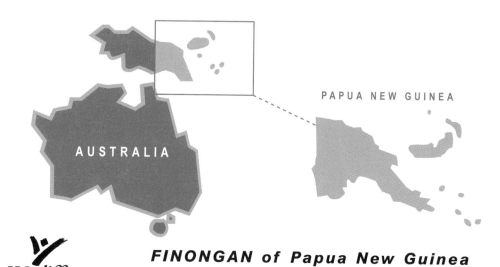

FINONGAN of Papua New Guinea
(Red)

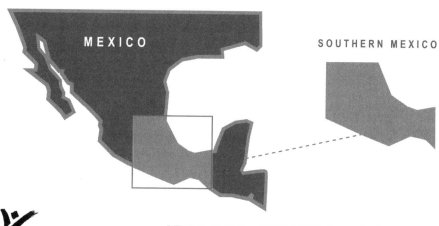

IPALAPA AMUZGO of Mexico
(Green)

LANGUAGE: NGULU
COUNTRY: TANZANIA

NGULU is also called KINGULU, NGURU, NGUU, WAYOMBA, and GEJA. The population is 132,000 (1987). They are located in east-central Tanzania, at about 37'E, between 5 and 7'S, at altitudes of 1,000 feet and higher. The area includes mountain slope, foothills, and plains.

NGULU belongs to the Bantu language family. The closest language linguistically is the 'Zigula' language. (It also needs a translation.) The NGULU of Tanzania is different from the Ngulu of Mozambique and Malawi.

The NGULU are a 'matrilineal' society. They practice their traditional religion. The people are traders, agriculturalists (growing maize, millet, sorghum, beans, peas, bananas, sugarcane, cassava, castor, peanuts, sweet potatoes, pumpkins, fruit, mountain rice, tobacco, cotton, and coffee), and practice animal husbandry (raising poultry, sheep, goats, and cattle).

There is a definite need for Bible translation into the NGULU language. Please pray for skilled workers for the task.

Bibleless Peoples, WBT • P.O. Box 2727 • Huntington Beach, CA 92647 • 1800-WYCLIFFE • www.Wycliffe.org

LANGUAGE: FINONGAN
COUNTRY: PAPUA NEW GUINEA

This language is also called FINUNGWAN and FINUNGWA. It belongs to the Trans-New Guinea language family. The population is 800 (1997 SIL). Speakers are located in Morobe Province's mountainous area.

The Lutheran and Evangelical Brotherhood Church (related to the Swiss Mission) contacted SIL in 1997, requesting a translation team be assigned. There is a definite need for translation into this language. Please pray for skilled workers for the task.

(Adapted from the 13th edition of the ETHNOLOGUE, Summer Institute of Linguistics.)

Bibleless Peoples, WBT • P.O. Box 2727 • Huntington Beach, CA 92647 • 1800-WYCLIFFE • www.Wycliffe.org

LANGUAGE: SANTA MARIA IPALAPA AMUZGO
COUNTRY: MEXICO

This language is also called IPALAPA AMUZGO. It belongs to the Oto-Manguean/Amuzgoan language family. The population is 1,200 including 60 monolinguals (1990 census). There may be up to 2,000 speakers, including more than 60 monolinguals (1992 C. Stewart SIL). Speakers are located in Mexico's State of Oaxaca, Putla District, about 8 to 10 miles northeast of San Pedro Amuzgos in five locations around Santa Maria Ipalapa. It is just off the highway from Tlaxiaco to the coast. SANATA MARIA IPALAPA AMUZGO is tonal and not intelligible with other Amuzgoan languages. Children grow up speaking the language. There is some bilingualism in Spanish. Primary and secondary education is available. As yet, there is no telephone or telegraph. This mountain slope and inland coastal area is at an altitude of 2,000 feet. It is savannah, with scrubs and gallery forests. The people are swidden agriculturalists, growing maize, beans, squash, chile peppers, and tomatoes.

Sufficient linguistic survey has been done to determine there is a definite need for Scripture translation in this language. Please pray for skilled workers for the task.

(Adapted from the 13th edition of the ETHNOLOGUE, Summer Institute of Linguistics.)

Bibleless Peoples, WBT • P.O. Box 2727 • Huntington Beach, CA 92647 • 1800-WYCLIFFE • www.Wycliffe.org